D0676781

ECONOMIC FREEDOM FOR THE WEST

WENDELL BERGE

ECONOMIC FREEDOM FOR THE WEST

UNIVERSITY OF NEBRASKA PRESS
LINCOLN • 1946 •

Printed in the United States by
STATE JOURNAL PRINTING COMPANY
LINCOLN

To the late

GEORGE W. NORRIS

valiant servant of the

American people

CONTENTS

FOREWORD

IT IS STILL too early to evaluate with precision the full significance of America's industrial achievement in World War II. Certain aspects of that accomplishment, however, have had a direct and startling effect upon our national life and our national thinking. The speed and capacity of our production not only unbalanced the plans of the Axis but also gave us a new conception of the vitality and the possibilities of our economic system. If we take full advantage of this insight there is every reason to believe that this nation can surpass in the years of peace ahead its performance under the pressure of war.

Historians have told us that the vanishing of the geographic frontier constituted a major turning point in our evolution. In a strict sense this was true, but all too often in the years before the war it was assumed that the passing of the geographic frontier also meant the disappearance of broad opportunities for economic development. The stark adversities of war compelled us to re-examine our economic potential and to recast our thinking. It soon became apparent that far from being mature or senile our economy had been asleep to its own powers, both in terms of technical progress and in terms of the fields awaiting exploration and enterprise.

Three basically important consequences emerged. First, sections of the country which had not been considered available or suitable for real industrial development suddenly became centers of war production and in some cases outstripped older communities. Second, scores of new industries began to manufacture new products using new techniques. Third, and even more important, was the recognition of the American people that our system of free enterprise has a tremendous capacity for future growth. It also became clear that among the principal factors responsible for slowing down the rate of our industrial advance has been the encroachment of monopolistic practices upon the functioning of enterprise and invention and upon the operation of the free market. Where monopoly had eliminated competition it had also eliminated opportunity.

Domestically it is our principal concern to demonstrate that our system of free enterprise can attain levels for production and employment which will provide rising standards of living for the American people and at the same time strengthen our economic and political liberties. The war has brought large industrial capacity to the West for the first time in history. Other sections of the country also developed war industries, but they had previously had large industrial capacity. The process of reconversion in the West, therefore, focuses more sharply than in any other section of the country the prob-

lems which our whole economy faces. In effect, the West has become the proving ground of free enterprise.

It is for this reason that the economic future of the West has a critical significance to the rest of the country. If the West is denied the chance to develop its resources, or if the South is not permitted to utilize new-found capabilities, then the East will also suffer. Our economy could not then look forward to expansion but would once more risk contraction and depression.

My underlying thought in writing this book is to demonstrate that the solution of these problems depends on keeping the channels of competitive opportunity open for local and regional industries; on promoting policies which will avoid monopoly and cartel control of the West's vast industrial potential. I believe that the chapters which follow will show that the problem is crucial and that its solution is vital to the health of our national economy. It is not a question of building up one region of the country as against another. It is rather an acceptance of the fact that our country cannot be prosperous if artificial and unnatural impediments are put in the way of each region's developing to the fullest its own industrial potential.

As Assistant Attorney General in charge of the Antitrust Division of the Department of Justice, I am constantly receiving complaints from all sections of the country involving alleged illegal restraints on free economic opportunity. These complaints usually come from businessmen who believe that the ganging-up of established companies to control a given field of business has prevented the complainants from developing their own independent enterprises.

The consideration of these complaints has taken me at one time or another to all parts of the country. I have had two occasions within the past year and a half to travel through the West and on both trips I have made a few speeches which dealt in a summary way with the theme which I have amplified in this book. A number of businessmen, publicists and others with whom I have had the opportunity to confer on these western trips suggested that I ought to expand them and incorporate them in a book. Shortly after a trip to the West Coast in the fall of 1944, the University of Nebraska Press invited me to develop the material of these speeches for publication. I agreed to undertake the project and had hoped that it would be completed much sooner. But the pressures of administering a large office which is actively on the firing line most of the time were such that it has taken considerably longer than I had expected to complete the book.

Most of the facts on which I have relied are taken from sources that are of public record, and they are listed in a bibliography on page 167.

For assistance in the preparation of this book I am primarily indebted to Dr. Charles A. Welsh, *Consulting Economist on the staff of the Antitrust Division. Dr. Welsh is one of my principal advisors on antitrust problems. His capacity for patient and painstaking research is boundless. His judgment on the significance of economic materials is exceptional. He is one of the outstanding men in the*

Antitrust Division, and I cannot praise too highly the splendid contribution he is making to the public service.

I also have relied upon Dr. George P. Comer, *Chief of the Economic Section of the Antitrust Division, for a great deal of valuable factual data. Dr. Comer is a veritable encyclopedia of industrial information. His capacity to direct me immediately to the sources of whatever information I have needed has been invaluable. I have also been helped by Dr. Comer's assistant,* Mrs. Lila G. Scott.

In administering a Division dealing with a field having as many ramifications and complexities as the economic field with which the Antitrust laws deal, I necessarily draw heavily for ideas and information on many members of my staff. In fact, it would be difficult for me to apportion credit with any degree of accuracy. In a broad sense I am indebted to the whole staff of the Antitrust Division for the outlook which I have tried to express in this book. The give and take of numerous staff conferences has done much to shape my thoughts on the questions I discuss on the following pages. I am particularly indebted to Joseph Borkin, *and I should also mention the splendid contributions of* Ward Bowman, *formerly a member of my staff and now a member of the Faculty of the University of Chicago Law School, and* Harold Wein *of the Antitrust Division staff, both of whom are experts on the steel industry.* Irving Lipkowitz *from time to time has given me great assistance in finding my way through the problems of the aluminum industry.* James E. Kilday *and* Frank L. Barton *have been particularly helpful to me in formulating the views which I have expressed on transportation problems.* Johnston Avery *has furnished some useful historical material.*

Miss Emily Schossberger, *of the University of Nebraska Press, has made many valuable suggestions and has been extremely cooperative in regard to the many details of publication.*

And there are many men and women in public and private life with whom I have been privileged from time to time to discuss current economic problems who have no doubt unconsciously made a contribution to this book. These include businessmen, lawyers, educators and newspapermen; local, state and federal government officials; and others too numerous to mention. I have benefited by these associations, but I take full responsibility myself for the views which I express. They are my own views, and I do not seek by these acknowledgments to attribute responsibility for them to any of the persons or groups to whom I have referred. And, of course, what I say does not purport to be an official expression of the views of the Department of Justice.

WENDELL BERGE

Washington, D. C.
March 26, 1946

"But Westward, look, the land is bright."

ARTHUR HUGH CLOUGH

CHAPTER 1

The West Comes of Age

THE United States has emerged among the victors in a war that encircled the world. American political institutions are unshaken. The principles of our freedom, defended by the lives and sacrifices of citizens from every level of society and every section of the country, are more firmly rooted than ever before in the consciousness of the people. Americans have vindicated their faith in the fundamental values of a free society. The basic soundness of American political democracy has never been more apparent than it is at the present time. Indeed thinking people the world over are coming more and more to the conviction that the American political structure presents the most promising pattern for future world organization to preserve the peace.

But what of the American economy? Here there is a deep and undeniable concern whether we shall succeed in creating a prosperity in which all parts of the country and all segments of the population will share the fruits of peace. It was as a nation that America engaged in its war effort. It must be as a nation that we achieve the economic objectives of peace. Until we do so there can be no enduring economic security for the country as a whole.

It is from this perspective that an approach to the problems of the West, or the South, or the East must be adopted. It has become imperative in this atomic age for us to divest our thinking of narrow nationalism in undertaking leadership for world peace. It is equally imperative that we outgrow the narrow sectionalism which long dominated the political and economic thought of the United States, and which exerted a warping influence upon our internal economic development. If we are to build a genuinely national prosperity there must be an adequate and continuing opportunity for all sections of the country to develop their own resources. Such development is necessary not only for each region itself, but so that the national economy will acquire a wider industrial base and a more stable foundation for the years ahead.

What is the West? Why should its problems concern the rest of the country? Land, people, freedom and enterprise are the words which contain the answers to these questions.

The West is land—fifteen immense states stretching from the Missouri River to the Pacific Ocean.[1] The West is a treasury of natural resources, the ac-

[1]The fifteen western states referred to are: Washington, Oregon, California, Nevada, Idaho, Montana, Wyoming, Utah, Colorado, Arizona, New Mexico, North Dakota, South Dakota, Nebraska and Kansas.

cumulated bounty of countless geological ages. Here are minerals of almost every variety and value; thousands of acres of rich and fertile earth; miles of flowing power in huge rivers. In national parks and in the lumber regions are great stands of forests. Even the vast wastes of desert and the "bad lands" which cover so much of the West seem to be nature's prodigious contrast to such prodigal gifts of wealth.

But the West is much more than land or climate or resources. The West is people and ideas—Americans whose thoughts and habits partake of the setting in which they have been shaped. Ordinarily when we think of the West we think of the age of pioneers. It is with the exploration and settlement of the West that we associate many of the most stirring episodes of our history. It is the spirit of the western frontier which we identify most directly with the growth of the nation to continental size. The lives and experience of the people who tamed the wilderness and finally reached the Pacific have become a legend and a heritage.

The men and women of several generations who first turned west and made the long trek across the continent were among the freest people who have ever lived. Their energies were exceeded only by their opportunities. Those who have come after them have drawn on the patrimony of the land, but even more have they taken their light from the sparks of optimism and progress which the early settlers bequeathed. America is still a young country, but nowhere in its borders is this sense of freedom and activity more palpable to the observer than it is in the West.

Like the essential traditions of American society itself, the traditions of the West are not fragile museum pieces, or cherished fragments of ancient glories and departed grandeur which fade and crumble into dust when exposed to light and air. Rather, the traditions of the West are a hardy, living group of attitudes and institutions derived from the long practice of liberty. Frontier life was often crude and lusty but it was intensely democratic. Both the sweeping contours of nature and the conditions of existence were forceful and dramatic. They made progressive vision a necessary trait of the people as a whole.

These same elements, refined and compounded by experience, compose the point of view of the modern West. It is the spirit of the frontier which has given western industry its air of dash and drive. The stupendous engineering of the Bonneville, Grand Coulee, or Boulder dams, or the scope and speed of production in shipyards and aircraft plants symbolize the West today as truly as any mining center represented it seventy-five years ago. No better criterion of the continued vigor of frontier democracy could be found than the economic contributions which the Western States have made to victory in the war.

If it has seemed in the past that the East and the South have not realized vividly enough how directly the fate of the West concerns them, it is only because a sufficiently dramatic occasion has been lacking to crystallize the unanimity of their interests. The end of the war is that occasion. The recognition of the problems of the West is now compelled by events.

Why? Because the future economic development of the West is a mirror which will focus and reflect the success or failure of our system of free enterprise. The whole tremendous struggle which is taking place in our economy between the forces of monopoly and free enterprise converges upon the issue of new competitive industry. Its outcome will determine whether there will be free markets, plentiful opportunity for initiative, a steady and satisfying demand for workers, more and better products for the American people at lower prices, and steadily rising standards of living.

The West is the arena in which the lines of this conflict are most explicitly marked and the contesting influences thrown into boldest relief. In the fight of Westerners to enter new peacetime branches of production, to increase their output, to multiply opportunities and to engage in competition in fields that have heretofore been closed to them, the people of the East and the South can gauge their own chances for an expanding realm of economic freedom. The same power of monopoly which tries to impose high prices and restricted production, leading ultimately to unemployment, upon eastern industry also seeks to stifle the possibility of new enterprise in the West. The same obstacles which hamper the free movement of goods from one part of the country to another prevent the fullest use of resources in all areas. The same type of discrimination which denies the West the chance to operate its own independent industries also compels the East and the South to deal with monopoly on its own terms, and to pay a tax to private privilege in the form of lessened purchasing power, fewer jobs, and narrowed markets.

The ability of the West to go forward is consequently one of the central issues of this postwar period in America's domestic affairs. If the portents now discernible are accurate in their prophecy, the economic future of the West is bright, not only because Westerners will capitalize to the utmost the opening which the end of the war has brought to them, but also because other sections of the country have learned in the past few years that their own welfare cannot be advanced to the maximum unless the West, the South, and the East develop together.

Free enterprise is the key which can unlock the combination of resources, people, markets and new industries for the West. Monopoly, in all of its overt and hidden forms and in all of its retarding effects, is the barrier which must be pierced before development can occur. In this conflict there can be no question that the West will have the active encouragement of people everywhere.

One of the principal effects of the war upon American life has been a great internal migration. Not since the days when men gravitated to the gold-fields has there been such an upheaval of population as that set in motion by these years of war. In the course of their duties in the armed services millions of men and women have left the communities in which they were born and had lived. These men and women travelled, often for the first time in their lives, from one end of the country to the other. Millions more have moved across the country to serve in war industries. Easterners have come in direct contact with the West. People from the Middle West have moved to the Eastern Seaboard or to the Pacific Coast. As is nearly always the case, this intermingling has broken down many of the traditional barriers and sectional differences in outlook.

In effect, this transcontinental flow of population during the period of the war has made Americans more aware than ever before of the interdependence of all areas of our economy. Not only have they come to recognition of where and how the economic interests of one region converge into those of another, but they have also come to recognize the way in which the geographical setting of economic problems produces differences in economic points of view. In other words, while acquiring a clearer understanding of the special circumstances of regions outside their own particular communities they have at the same time gained a wider conception of our whole economic system. This realization of the economic unity of the country will undoubtedly prove to be a most fortunate influence in the future of the West.

To appreciate fully the transformation which has occurred within the years immediately past it is necessary to contrast the traditional portrait of the West with the realities of the present. Certainly it is now necessary to revise the outworn picture of the Western States as areas barren of industrial development or possibilities for such development. The truth of the matter is that during the war years the West has come of age industrially. The energy and initiative of Western industrialists in creating and expanding plants and facilities to produce ships, planes, and numerous other war supplies aroused national admiration. The zest, skill and determination with which Western workers and technicians performed their tasks set a pace for the entire country. The great storehouse of raw materials in the West opened and poured out its wealth of mineral, forest, farm, and factory products to supply a large part of national war needs.

The barest facts of the war performance of the fifteen Western states are impressive. They built several billion dollars worth of war plants. From the beginning of the national emergency through April, 1945, the West filled contracts for war supplies valued at twenty-nine billions of dollars—an amount five times more than the value of all manufactured products from the area in 1939.

Now the war is over, and all areas of our economy are in various stages of reconversion. In many respects there is no section of the country where the difficulties involved in redirecting industry from war to peace are as complex and challenging as they are in the West. In the aftermath of war it seems at times as though these problems are baffling and insuperable.

Reconversion, however, is only a partial and temporary phase of transition. In a broader and deeper perspective it is apparent that there are certain fundamental considerations which must be taken into account because they will largely determine the economic position of the West in the long run. It is in the light of basic principles and clear objectives that the West must make decisions on economic policy.

The swift construction and amazing productivity of war industries in the West have given us a glimpse of what long-run developments can be. The war supplies produced there included large quantities of ships, planes, foodstuffs, mineral products, chemicals, light metals and a host of other goods which before the war were produced in the West only in moderate amounts or not at all.

What is important, however, is that these plants and their enormous output have demonstrated beyond argument what the West can do. The same qualities of creative imagination and enterprise, managerial ability and craftsmanship which successfully constructed and operated entirely new industries for war purposes can provide an excellent foundation for the industrialization of the West. Many organizations which were born during the war years will be able to use their equipment and know-how to enter new fields. This is true not only of the great war plants; it is true also of the numerous small factories and going concerns which the war brought into being. They will have the support of a trained and intelligent working population eager to partake in industrial development.

For the West, as for our whole national economy, the aims of full production and full employment must be major guides to policy. As a people we cannot be content with any less than the highest standard of living which our industrial system has shown to be within our grasp. We cannot permit a repetition of the "boom and bust" prosperity which collapsed into depression after the last war. We cannot tolerate mass unemployment and the lack of opportunity for individuals and for enterprise.

It is at this point that the economic future of the West assumes a special significance for the country as a whole. It is not possible for prosperity to continue very long in one part of the economy if other parts are depressed, unable to expand their output and consequently unable to increase their volume of consumption or to raise their standards of living. The national volume of production and the national income cannot rise to higher levels unless the potential output of the West is turned to account. The national market cannot be firmly sustained unless the ability of the West to obtain the things it needs and wants is also sustained.

Far from injuring the interests of other sections, the rise of Western industry will substantially abet their economic effectiveness. It will do so not only by extending the domain of competition, but by furthering the healthy decentralization of many industries. Whatever short-run adjustments are encountered along the way, there can be no question that the competitive spreading of industry not only stimulates economic activity in general, but in time yields far higher returns in the way of new avenues for capital investment, more and better-paid jobs, and the multiplied exchange of goods among the several regions. The United States lives on a continent. Its continental economy will be most strongly balanced when all of its parts have acquired an internal harmony of development which permits their smooth and automatic integration. This is the true object of free enterprise.

There are further equally important considerations which merit attention. The United States now has responsibilities in shaping and maintaining a healthy world economy. A firm economic basis is needed for our participation in world affairs. We cannot allow our industrial strength to be diluted.

On the contrary, our industrial power which provided the winning margin in the battle of production against the Axis must be continued, and even increased, to correspond to our role in making peace secure. From this standpoint the Western industries are a major addition to our industrial potential.

Aside from the beneficial effects on the whole national economy of decentralizing some basic industries, it is in the foremost national interest to preserve the productive power of the West as an asset of freedom. It would be tragic irony, as well as a blunder, if these facilities built for the purpose of defending democracy against aggression were not utilized to promote the welfare and security of democracy in peace.

The conditions which are necessary to the attainment of an enduring prosperity in the West are more sharply visible, in some ways, than in any other part of the country. Similarly, the threats and obstacles to development are more apparent. If the inherent wealth which the West possesses is to be utilized in production, not only must the adaptable war industries be transferred to a sound peacetime basis, but new industries must emerge. To bring this development about will not be easy. It will require foresight, energy, resourcefulness and cooperation.

In viewing the panorama of prospects and possibilities certain broad questions stand out. What is the economic future of the West to be? How can the West transform its rich natural endowment and its great potential capacities into economic accomplishments? What role is the West able and entitled to play in an expanding and balanced national economy and beyond that in the world economy? What obstacles must be met in order for the West to achieve its fullest desirable growth? What measures are available to surmount these hazards?

In briefest form, our point of departure is the question: Where does the West go from here? In pursuing an answer, I believe it will be possible not only to define some of the elements which are responsible for retarding the growth of the West in the past but also to obtain some rather accurate indications of the direction which must be sought if the West is to reach its rightful economic stature and to acquire full partnership in the national economy. In the course of this survey it will become evident that by any route the way is not easy, and is indeed beset with difficulties. It will also become clear that all the means of action, all the incentives and all the opportunities necessary to the achievement of these goals are abundantly present.

CHAPTER II

Economic Transition

SOMEONE has pertinently observed that the great war plants have opened a new frontier in American economic development. This is especially true for the West. In the past the West has lacked factory and plant facilities. Now it has hundreds of them scattered over all the vast area from the Missouri River to the Pacific Ocean.

There is, however, a pressing question concerning the fate of these war plants. To the West the suddenness of victory brought the full impact of reconversion so that the West is confronted both with the problems of the present—the closing of many plants—and at the same time the consideration of long range factors which will affect permanent industrial development.

It will be necessary as we go along to refer in some detail to particular war expenditures made in Western States. Some preliminary facts, however, may be helpful, in orienting our thinking and in comprehending the scope of the issues involved.

The total war plant facilities built from June, 1940, through December, 1944, amounted to something over twenty-one billion dollars ($21,000,000,000) of which the Government supplied sixteen billion dollars ($16,000,000,000) and private enterprise about five billion dollars ($5,000,000,000). Of the total facilities the fifteen states of the West have war plants valued at about three billion one hundred and thirty million dollars ($3,130,000,000). Slightly less than two billion four hundred and seventy-five million dollars ($2,475,000,000) was supplied by public funds and about six hundred and fifty-six million dollars ($656,000,000) by private funds.

In effect, these facilities represent a drastic and far-reaching change in the economic position of the West. The contrast is especially striking if we compare the picture as it is now with the situation which existed only a few years ago. Before the war the West was far behind the country as a whole in the value of its industrial products. In 1939, manufacturing industries in the United States produced approximately fifty-seven billion dollars ($57,000,000,000) worth of goods. Factory products of the Western States were valued at about five and one-half billion dollars ($5,500,000,000) or less than 10% of the total for the country.

It is possible to define the crux of the economic problem of the West as it was at that time in terms of a few figures. The fifteen Western States contained roughly 50% of the land area of the country. In 1939, however, they had only 14% of the population, 8% of the factory employment and 10% of the value of factory products out of the national totals.

It is against this background that we must measure the progress which has already been made. Quite clearly the problem of the West is not only to prevent these gains from being dissipated, but to add to them the elements required for economic balance. This means that as far as possible the war industries must be kept going to produce articles of peacetime trade. It means that Western capital must have an opportunity not only to continue in industries already established but must also be able to enter new fields.

It is especially necessary to keep in mind the character of the period through which this country is now passing. The national economy is in a phase of transition from war to peace, but in a climate of opinion and an environment of circumstances which are far different from the aftermath of the First World War. At that time the desire for a return to "normalcy" overrode every other consideration without much thought being given to the economic trends which were present. At first all seemed well, but in retrospect it is painfully obvious that the same momentum which bore us to the crest of a brief prosperity also carried us crashing into depression.

Today people are concerned with economic causes and effects. They realize that the dangers and difficulties of economic policy can be disregarded only at the peril of depression. What is most encouraging, however, is the resurgence of a desire to see the system of free enterprise function as we know it can. There is a reawakened conviction that a free economy can provide the largest "elbow room" of opportunity for the individual if the conditions which fetter opportunity are removed. It is by this healthy, active and progressive public opinion, as much as by specific acts of Government, that confidence in ability to cope with the future is created.

These forces of opinion are further reflected in a new kind of regionalism which has stirred nearly every corner of the country. Regional abilities not previously recognized, as well as some which had been long dormant were released during the years of the war. At the same time this regionalism is no longer the result of accentuated differences but rather a progressive desire on the part of those who live in the various sections of the country to develop the best possible qualities and aspects of their environment in order to participate more effectively in the larger life of the nation.

Relatively speaking, the prospects that we shall be able to maintain a steadily expanding economy are much more favorable today than in 1919, not because the difficulties are fewer, but because the American people are aware of them and are imbued with a realistic attitude which acknowledges problems but emphasizes progress. Primarily, this attitude stems from the fundamental belief that our economic system is entirely capable of fulfilling the high promise which our history has held forth.

Along with the East and the South, the West now shares a chance which does not come often in history, to start afresh the process of economic freedom. To the West, intelligent regionalism of this order means not only a far greater degree of local economic autonomy; it means the reconstitution of a point of view, the recapture of the spirit of adventure in economic affairs. This is not an undertaking in which the West and the East are pitted against each other. Only those who speak the language of monopoly can think of it in such terms. Rather, a vital Western regionalism will have as its premise the understanding that it is part of a joint enterprise in which the country as a whole will lose if the West is held down, but in which the entire nation will benefit as the West is able to develop.

The character of needed change is partially obvious from the cycle which Western trade ordinarily follows. Many of the raw materials of American industry are produced west of the Missouri River, shipped East for processing, and then shipped back again to Western markets. A large part of the financing of Western raw material industries has been done by a comparatively few great bankers of the East. Even the railroads of the West and their communications systems have been largely managed from Eastern centers. It is not meant to imply that there was at first anything deliberate in the colonial treatment of the West by Eastern financiers and industrial interests. Historically, new lands are always developed in this manner. In the pioneering stage foreign capital is essential, but after nearly a century maturity is expected. When a mature degree of independence is not forthcoming it gradually becomes clear that something is economically wrong.

That this pattern of Western trade is cut principally from the past is evident from a single example. In a classic of American literature, *Two Years Before The Mast,* Richard Henry Dana, almost one hundred years ago, gave a fascinating report on the hide-curing business as it was then conducted. After making the tortuous trip around Cape

Horn and collecting hides from various ports on the West Coast, he pointed out that "They were carried to Boston, tanned, made into shoes . . . brought back again to California . . . and worn in pursuit of other bullocks, or in curing of other hides." And still today this same sort of transit goes on with many Western products. Wool bought at Portland auctions in normal times travels five or six thousand miles around through the Canal to Boston where it is worked into fabrics, moved back to Rochester for manufacture into men's suits, and shipped west to consumers. Copper is produced in the West and shipped to the Connecticut Valley for processing. It returns to the West in the form of wire and cable for use, perhaps, at Bonneville, Grand Coulee, or elsewhere—approximately where it started.

Rather than beginning with a complete inventory of the resources of the Western States I believe it will be more realistic to examine some of the industries which the West now has and to draw attention to those fields which will afford the greatest room for expansion. In doing so it should be understood that not all of the war plants can reasonably be expected to survive the peace, particularly those producing arms and munitions. Our concern is the degree to which industries capable of reconversion will be given a fair chance and the degree to which opportunity will be accorded for new industries to emerge.

There are, of course, numerous types of industrial expansion which have taken place within the past five or six years. Although every industry will meet its own unique problems, throughout all of them the underlying difficulties encountered are likely to be much the same in character. In some cases there may be natural handicaps which can only gradually be overcome by intelligent management. In many more, however, it will be the pattern of artificial hindrances, of restraints and discriminations, of monopolistic practices and cartel controls, which must be fought.

The expansion which has occurred in any field cannot continue if it is caught in an economic pincers between the pressure of monopoly groups in other parts of the country, discriminatory costs of transportation, or the exclusion of products from world markets by cartel agreements. In discussing such adverse factors as basing point systems, patent abuses or cartel restrictions in one industry, it should be borne in mind that they apply with equal effect to many others. It should be pointed out also that the trade restraints which Western industry will encounter are largely inherited from the past and that they are reviewed not for the purpose of condemning them on a moral basis but simply because there can be no solution to the problems of the West if such practices persist.

CHAPTER III

Western Steel

EVEN in our rapidly changing industrial system, in which new resources and new processes are constantly introduced, steel continues to be the foundation of industrial development. It is therefore an economic event of the first magnitude that there is now a sizeable steel industry in the West which is completely integrated from raw materials to finished products.

Before the war the bulk of all steel consumed in the Western States was shipped several thousand miles by rail and water to Pacific ports and then moved inland to its final destination. The annual consumption of steel in the fifteen Western States in the prewar years amounted to some 3,000,000 tons, 75% of which was used by consumers on the Pacific Coast.[1]

[1]The 3,000,000 tons consumed in the West were distributed approximately as follows: the Pacific Coast States took about 2,250,000 tons, the Mountain States took about 600,000 tons, and the Plains States accounted for the remainder, something under 200,000 tons.

Some steel was produced west of the Rockies before the war by open hearth furnaces using steel scrap and some pig iron most of which was shipped from Provo, Utah. Total productive capacity was about 1,000,000 tons but there was complete dependence upon outside sources for such important products as tin plate, pipes and tubes, and cold rolled sheet and strip. By 1944, however, steel ingot capacity had expanded 3½ times, attaining a level of some 3,500,000 tons. This does not include the capacity of 1,200,000 tons of the Colorado Fuel & Iron Corporation at Pueblo, Colorado.

Steel-making facilities west of the Rocky Mountains capable of producing 3½ million tons of ingots represent a potential producing capacity of about 2½ million tons of steel finished products. (There is an estimated conversion loss of 30% from ingots to finished products.) This figure balances very closely with the amount of steel consumed in the seven far western states in 1937. For the rest of the country the equivalent ratio of 1944 capacity to 1937 shipments was slightly greater than 3 to 2. As this was a relatively depressed period, the comparison is very conservative. In fact, if steel consumption in the West were to tap its potential postwar market to the full, it is estimated that capacity would fall below rather than exceed demand. This is not to imply that there are not very real difficulties ahead in maintaining, balancing and expanding a new steel industry in the West. It should, however, dispel the oft-repeated but illusory cry of excess capacity concerning Western steel.

The real problems are to be found elsewhere.[2] Most of the greatly increased steel-making capacity in the West is accounted for by two newly added integrated steel-making plants—the Government-owned steel producing plant at Geneva, Utah, and the Kaiser plant at Fontana, California. The latter, although not Government-owned, has been largely financed by Government loan. Together these plants represent almost two million tons of steel-ingot capacity. Their finishing facilities, however, are restricted principally to products required by a wartime shipbuilding industry. The most important of these products are plates and structural shapes, the postwar Western demand for which can make up only a very small proportion of the wartime producing capacity. Consequently, a substantial reconversion job is needed to fit Western producing capacity to Western needs if the new industry is to survive and prosper. This will involve essentially new investment.

Western business and industrial interests are especially concerned with the future operations of the newly added steel facilities. This concern as expressed by the Western States Council, a representative group of Western business and professional leaders, points up the Western steel problem. This problem is twofold. First, there is a definite need for accelerating the industrial development of the West to provide better balance between industry,

[2]Even though the Colorado Fuel and Iron Corporation in Pueblo has not utilized a substantial part of its producing capacity over a great number of non-war years it should be pointed out that this plant is farther freight-wise from the principal Wes'ern markets than are Eastern Seaboard producers. Also its principal market outlet is the sale of rails and railroad supplies to railroad companies.

agriculture and commerce, and to provide jobs for industrial workers who came to the West from all parts of the country during the war. A substantial proportion of these jobs can be provided through expansion of the metal fabricating industry, producing such items as steel girders for buildings, steel bars for the automobile industry, steel pipe and tubing, steel wire, and tin plate. In the past this industry has fallen short of its potential, because in no small measure, the high price of steel in the West has inhibited its growth.

As the Western Council also points out, the price for different types of steel in the Western markets has reflected the basing point price in the Eastern steel-producing centers plus an amount which is approximately equal to transportation costs from Atlantic or Gulf ports. The Pacific Coast price, for example, has in general been from $10 to $15 more per ton than in the Eastern producing centers. These higher prices have been paid by Western buyers of steel not only for steel produced in Eastern mills, but also for steel produced in the West.

This prevalence of the basing point system underscores a type of obstacle with which much of Western industry has had to contend for many years. Under this system in the past the prices of various steel products have been quoted at a few base mills, all of which were east of the Mississippi River. To these base prices the cost of freight to the point of consumption is then added. By means of this formula the price of steel at any delivery point in the United States is set at exactly the same figure, regardless of the point from which the steel is shipped. Thus when a contractor in Omaha asked for quotations on steel, he would be given, under the basing point system, precisely the same figure from all suppliers whether they are located in Chicago, Kansas City or Pueblo, Colorado. He would also discover that the price of steel products made by a mill in, let us say, Pueblo, was not a Pueblo mill price but rather a Chicago mill price to which had been added the cost of transport by rail from Chicago to the Pueblo mill. In other words, because Pueblo was not a basing point its prices would be governed by the nearest base in the Chicago area. Even though the steel might be shipped from Colorado, its cost to the ultimate consumer would include a "phantom freight" charge as though it had been shipped from Chicago.

The abuses of the basing point system have affected the West in many industries, most notably in steel, petroleum products, sugar, and cement. In this connection, the Report of Attorney General Biddle to Congress on Western steel plants and the tin plate industry stated that the elimination of monopolistic control from the East, including the basing point system, constituted one of the most important conditions to be met in providing a basis for large-scale Western operations.[3]

The existence of integrated steel-making capacity in the West was only accomplished through the excessive wartime demand for steel. Consequently the question arises as to why such capacity was not previously installed in the West. Many reasons have been advanced to account for this retarded de-

[3]Report of the Attorney General of the United States on *Western Steel Plants and The Tin Plate Industry*, under Section 205 of the War Mobilization and Reconversion Act, June, 1945.

velopment. These include the economies of large scale production in Eastern centers, the thinness of the market in the West, the relatively low cost of shipping steel from the East in company-owned vessels, the existence of a large amount of unutilized steel capacity in the East, the economies of adding to existing facilities as against building new facilities in new areas, and the inadequacy of raw materials in the West.

Numerous attempts have been made to establish independent integrated steel producing facilities in the West. These attempts have extended over a period of some thirty years. The lack of success of these ventures has been ascribed to somewhat different reasons, however, than those mentioned above. In a report for the Corps of Engineers, Edwin T. Hodge, consulting geologist, stated in 1935 that although the market for steel in the West was of sufficient size and raw materials were available at a cost capable of meeting Eastern competition the failure to establish a Western steel industry was attributable to other factors. He stated: "No doubt the primary cause of failure was the temerity of capital, especially in fear of influences, other than strict business economics."[4]

Another eminent geologist, C. K. Leith, is quoted as stating in 1929 that "On the West Coast of the United States there are raw materials for an iron and steel industry and there has been discussion for years as to the possibilities of starting a large-scale

[4]Hodge, Edwin T., *Available Raw Materials for Pacific Coast Iron Industry*, page 18, War Department, Corps of Engineers, Office of Division Engineer, North Pacific Division, Portland, Oregon, October 15, 1935.

steel industry. The consuming power of the local population for all kinds of iron and steel would seem to be great enough to warrant such action.'"[5]

On August 6, 1942, a Mr. Henry J. Landahl, Secretary-Treasurer of the Pacific-American Steel Iron Corporation, Bellingham, Washington, testified before the Truman Committee as follows:[6]

> Historically the effort to create an iron and steel industry on the Pacific Coast has been undertaken on many occasions in the last thirty years, efforts in which the officers and directors of our Corporation have participated and in which they have invested substantial sums of money and a great deal of time and effort. There has never been a question of the feasibility of an iron and steel industry in this area, but on each occasion when the efforts have been made to establish an industry, the planning and work of those engaged in the project has been frustrated through connivance and intervention on the part of existing steel corporations and existing financial combinations.

Subsequently Mr. Landahl referred to a letter, written in 1922, which he had received from Vickers, Ltd. of Great Britain, stating: ". . . we foresee the possibility of this scheme being hindered in its operation through the action of the U. S. Steel Corp. and we feel that we should have more information as regards their views for or against this proposal."

Senators O'Mahoney, Truman and Kilgore felt called upon to comment as follows:

> Senator O'Mahoney: It seems to me that the last paragraph as I was about to say is a very eloquent testimonial to the manner in which the large group oper-

[5] *Ibid.*, p. 31.
[6] Hearings before the Special Committee Investigating the National Defense Program (Truman Committee), Part 14, p. 5839.

ates internationally to restrain development and concentrate control throughout the world of the natural resources upon which the lives of the people depend.

The Chairman: (Senator Truman) It fits into the aluminum and Standard Oil group procedure, all of which we have had right before the Committee. This is just another link in the same chain.

Senator Kilgore: It is a sort of unwritten cartel.[7]

Regardless of what the reasons have been for the lack of development of Western steel producing facilities the existence of basic steel making capacity is now an accomplished fact. Furthermore, studies by Government agencies, the Western Steel Committee, several recognized engineering firms, and private steel companies themselves indicate that both of the new large scale steel producing plants in the West (Geneva and Fontana) can be operated by private owners on a basis which will show a reasonable profit to operations and at the same time reduce the price differential which Western steel buyers have had to pay. There are, however, two important "ifs" plus the necessity for a careful distinction between "can" and "will."

The first "if" relates to the amount and terms which the Government will exact for its property. Overhead costs are an extremely important element of total costs in the steel industry. This fact, together with the fact that substantial new investment is required to fit wartime plants to postwar uses makes it essential that new operators not be saddled with excessive overheads. Primary consideration must be given to prospective earnings in determining the sale or lease value of Government-owned

[7] *Ibid.*, p. 5912.

plants. The Surplus Property Administrator has recognized the importance of this point in his iron and steel report to the Congress. Consequently, there is reason to hope that financing arrangements with the Government will take adequate cognizance of this same fact. It is now rather generally understood that the West cannot expect to benefit fully from competition until excessive financial overheads are reduced.

The second "if" pertains to the railroad freight rates from the Geneva, Utah plant to West Coast markets. It is of basic importance that these rates reflect the competitive advantage of location at Geneva by bearing logical relationship to transportation costs which exist from this area to the Coast on ore, pig iron, and cast iron pipe, all of which have moved from the Utah region. This means that freight rates on finished steel products cannot be maintained at a level more than twice as high as freight rates on pig iron or iron ore. Obviously, high transportation rates for finished steel from Geneva to the West Coast where 75% of the Western steel market exists is a vital limiting factor, since no commercial rates have as yet been established.

It would seem reasonable to assume that the two qualifications which have been noted can be adequately disposed of with proper diligence. With respect to the question of excessive overhead cost, the policy as set down by the Surplus Property Administration lends real support. With respect to freight rates, although the result will depend on the bargaining power of the Geneva plant, a hopeful sign in this connection is that principal Geneva competition can be expected from inter-coastal water-borne traffic. Under these conditions, the railroads may find it to their interest to divert as much traffic as possible to the rail haul from Geneva.

But a very vital problem to the Western steel consumer still remains. How will the consumer be assured of lower steel prices which will allow Western fabricating industries to expand? There was a modest, but respectable steel industry in the West before the war, which in 1940 produced some 750,000 tons of steel products. Almost all of the output was priced to Western consumers in exactly the same manner and at the same level as if it had been produced in the East. What is to keep this same pricing pattern from being continued into the postwar period, especially if the same major Eastern interests get control of the new Western plants? The West has every right to expect vigorous independent competitive pricing of the steel products which it buys. The West owes a great deal to the independent initiative of its early pioneers. It would benefit immeasurably now if a few pioneers in the field of steel pricing could succeed in establishing competitive conditions.

Speed in getting under way is an important consideration in the future of Western steel. The large Eastern producers have already indicated that as postwar markets develop they will expand the scope of their operations, and their plans are in some instances already active. With the passage of time the chances for the establishment of an independent Western steel industry would consequently become less. To become effective large scale production of steel in the West should therefore begin at the earliest possible moment.

Steel is a magnetic industry. It makes jobs. It fulfills and creates demands for other industries, through its needs, its products, the capital it requires, and the purchasing power it expends. Without substantial steel production, other types of manufacture cannot get started in the West. With steel as a center of gravity, other industries will be drawn into the orbit of Western markets. To electrify this magnet of steel is the principal task confronting Western enterprise.

CHAPTER IV

Western Aluminum

SEVENTY-FIVE per cent of the weight of an airplane is made up of one material—aluminum. Standing alone, this fact reveals the importance of the aluminum industry. We have only to recall the collections of aluminum scrap when this country entered the war to realize that aluminum is the primary metal of airpower. But the peacetime uses of aluminum, in commercial planes, modern trucks, buses, automobiles, railroad trains, transmission lines, household utensils, and "gadgets" of every variety can be many times what they were up to Pearl Harbor. One use of aluminum is particularly important in the immediate future as structural material for houses. The use of aluminum for prefabricated homes is already under way in Canada.

There are a score of industries in which aluminum has already been introduced or in which it will be introduced, provided that the aluminum industry is competitive in its structure and active in marketing its wares to industrial and individual consumers.

These considerations lead to Western aluminum. War demands and Government action have resulted in the establishment of an aluminum industry in the West. What is to become of it?

Unless we have a clear and controlling public policy on the matter the aluminum plants of the West will either be closed down or they will fall into the control of the Aluminum Company of America. In the latter event they would not likely continue in production. There is no moral censure of the Aluminum Company in saying that with its plants scattered all over the East, the South and the West it will operate only those which promise the greatest profit. When an industry is monopolistic in character, such a formula is a part of the rules of the game. Management in such a case cannot be expected to do anything else but to follow the logic of its position. Possessing great plants at all the more suitable water power sites throughout the country, and possessing a superior position with respect to control of the basic raw material, bauxite, Alcoa is well fortified, and its advantages are many.

All of us are familiar with the pattern of monopoly under which the American aluminum industry has operated for so long. Prior to the war a single producer dominated the field. In fact, for forty years the Aluminum Company of America supplied more than 90% of all the aluminum consumed in the United States, taking into account imports which it did not control. Before the war Alcoa produced 100% of the domestic output of virgin aluminum. During the war the total productive capacities were multiplied seven times, primarily by the use of Government funds, but Alcoa operated all but one of the public plants and all but two of the private plants. At the present time all types of plants, including both those in operation and those in a "standby" status, have an annual ingot capacity of 1,880,000,000 pounds. As late as September, 1945, Alcoa had control of approximately 90% of the total. This does not take into account capacity owned by the Government, but not held in operating condition, of more than 500,000,000 pounds.

Six major Western plants are now in existence—four of them in Washington, one in California, and one in Oregon. These Western plants have a combined aluminum ingot capacity of nearly 820,000,000 pounds annually or more than two and one-half times the average annual consumption of aluminum in the whole of the United States before the war. In the five years from 1935 to 1940 the average annual consumption was approximately 316,000,000 pounds, which is nearly 40% of the present capacity of the Western plants alone.

These plants cost a lot of money. The one at Spokane cost the Government twenty-three million dollars ($23,000,000); at Torrance, California, nearly twenty-five million dollars ($25,000,000); and at Troutdale, Oregon, about nineteen million dollars ($19,000,000). There is, therefore, a total Government investment in Western aluminum ingot plants (including a smaller plant operated by the Olin Corporation) of nearly seventy-five million dollars ($75,000,000). Added to this figure are Government loans made to private companies, so that there is a very large total Government investment in Western aluminum plants. Again, it would be possible to add the value of fabricating facilities to these figures to reach even more enormous totals. For example, there is a sheet mill at Spokane which cost the Government more than forty-seven million dollars ($47,000,000). In round figures, therefore, the Government has not much less than two hundred million dollars ($200,000,000) in Western aluminum plants.

It is not possible to trace all of the ramifications or all of the intricate issues which stem from the question raised by this huge investment. It must be recognized, however, that the character of the policies adopted in the aluminum industry and the success with which decisions are carried out will affect not simply the reconversion period but will also have an intimate bearing upon the future of all Western industry. It is generally agreed that although the demand for aluminum for some time will not attain the proportions of wartime consumption, because of the slackening in aircraft production, the ultimate market for the metal will be much greater than it ever was before the war. The trend to light metals, especially in new industries, is accelerating for two reasons. First, the light metals as a group are especially adaptable by industrial users from a cost standpoint. Secondly, individual consumers are particularly responsive to light metal products because they are sturdy without being cumbersome and because they can be shaped and colored in ways that are not economically feasible with other materials.

It is agreed also that the establishment of competition in the aluminum industry is a test of economic policy which must be met if we are not to invite once more the domination of the field by monopoly. In September, 1945, Attorney General Clark submitted for the consideration of the Congress his recommendations concerning the best means of bringing about healthy competition in the aluminum industry.[1] In general these recommendations and the facts upon which they are based set forth at length the conditions which must be sought if competition with a minimum of Government participation is to operate in the aluminum industry by a self-sustaining process. A successful competitive solution of the problem of aluminum will not only make possible the survival and growth of a Western aluminum industry but will provide material for many new fabricating facilities to produce planes, household articles, and other aluminum products. In fact, a whole cluster of new auxiliary industries could be expected to grow up around aluminum, as its applications are explored.

One of the first questions, as well as one of the most difficult, in connection with the possibility of an independent Western aluminum industry is that of the relative cost of ingot production. Unfortunately, cost data are available to the public only with respect to Government-owned plants. Consequently, we do not know how low Alcoa's costs may have gone during the war or how low they may go under more normal operating conditions in peacetime. It would appear that on the basis of costs in Government plants, the West has a reasonable equality of position and advantage.

In the report made to Congress by the Attorney General, already cited, unit costs of plant operations are set forth in great detail and subdivided among

[1]"Report of the Attorney General under Section 205 of the War Mobilization and Reconversion Act of 1944" (Washington, D. C., September 11, 1945.)

the factors of raw material (alumina), power, labor, carbon electrodes, and similar items, together with the total cost before depreciation, general overhead, and taxes. Although these costs do not include all commercial items and are consequently not a complete index of probable postwar prices, they are significant because they show the relative positions of plants in various parts of the country. A few examples will clarify this relationship. Thus, for the year 1944 the total operating cost per pound of ingot at Jones Mill, Arkansas, was 11.9¢. At Los Angeles it was slightly above 13¢ per pound (through the month of August at which time it was closed). At Massena, New York, in the DPC plant, cost was approximately 15¢ per pound. Incidentally, there is reason to believe that Alcoa's private plant at Massena has substantially lower cost of production. In New York City, cost was about 15½¢ per pound; and at Burlington, New Jersey, it was in the neighborhood of 15¢.

Some of the Western plants, at least, showed lower cost figures than any of those cited above. The Troutdale, Oregon, plant showed an average for 1944 of 11.3¢ per pound and Spokane an even 11¢. The relatively small operations of Tacoma were reflected in costs of about 16¢ per pound.

Quite clearly, "pennies count" in the manufacture of aluminum, because cost differences as small as one-tenth of a cent per pound become dollars when we speak of tons. To the household consumer of coal, a rise or decrease of a dollar a ton is important. To the consumer of aluminum, a rise or decrease of a few dollars a ton may be the deciding factor in its use.

The key factor in aluminum production in the Columbia Basin is in the cost of power. This is apparent if we compare the operating cost at Jones Mill, Arkansas (11.9¢), which included a power cost of 4¢ per pound, with that at Troutdale, Oregon, where power costs only 2¢ per pound, or at Spokane where the power factor was 1.9¢ per pound. Where cost relationships are so important, an advantage of 2¢ on the power factor alone can be extremely important over any fairly long period.

But there are other important factors in aluminum production. For instance, the basic raw material, alumina, cost more during the war in the Western plants than elsewhere. The cost of alumina per pound of ingot at Jones Mill, Arkansas, ranged about 4.7¢ per pound; at Troutdale about 5.5¢ per pound. In other words, the 2¢ power advantage of the Western plants is counteracted by a disadvantage of 1¢ per pound in the cost of raw material. As Alcoa controls much of the high-grade domestic raw materials—that is the bauxite deposits in Arkansas and South America—the high cost to the Western plants is still an open question subject to review. In specific terms, if Western plants can obtain material on a competitive basis to be used with cheap power, they can survive the competition of Alcoa. Otherwise, the ability of the Western plants to operate is problematical, especially if we take into consideration the transportation charge on aluminum ingot shipped out of the Columbia Basin.[2]

There are, of course, many other questions in-

[2]A summary of the cost figures for Government aluminum plants for the year 1944 will be shown in Table No. 1, p. 153, in the Appendix.

volved in the survival of the Western aluminum industry. Frankly, it may be doubted whether a private company could operate a Western ingot plant alone and stay in business by selling the product on the open market. Such concerns would be extremely vulnerable to competition from Alcoa. It must be pointed out, also, that effective competition in fabrication depends upon effective competitive production of the metal. Fabricators purchasing ingot from Alcoa would be buying their supplies from their largest competitor.

It would seem that in order for independent competition to develop, independents would necessarily have to begin with raw material. This means that independent aluminum producers would have to own or control sources of bauxite or have access on equal terms to sources of the ore. They would need their own alumina plants in order to reduce four tons of bauxite to two tons of alumina. These requirements are, of course, over and above the necessary possession of the electrolytic ingot plants needed to reduce the two tons of alumina to one ton of aluminum. Indeed, the requirements of complete independence would actually go much farther. Independent operators would need to own sheet mills, rolling mills, wire mills and extrusion facilities in order to make their products available to fabricators.

If after this integration were accomplished at the cost of several millions of dollars, they could bring their prices within the range of automobile companies, aircraft producers and all of the many fabricators of aluminum, they would then have an equal chance of survival in competition with Alcoa. Obviously the road to independence is long and arduous. Nevertheless, it must inevitably be traversed unless we are willing to tolerate an aluminum monopoly during the next half century as we have in the past fifty years. These assertions, of course, are made as statements of simple fact without any implications beyond the premises of the antitrust laws.

It is in the cold light of these facets of the problem that a constructive solution must be sought. There is an element of urgency involved, for the sooner that action is taken at the outset of the post-war period, the sooner will the Western aluminum plants be able to begin the development of their large potential markets. Undue delay would be doubly harmful to these prospects not only from the standpoint of competitive production but also in the race for new consumers of aluminum.

Is there any answer to this dilemma? Although other suggestions have been put forward, and further fruitful proposals will undoubtedly be made, the recommendations contained in the report of the Attorney General cited above offer solid ground for discussion. In the letter of the Attorney General submitting the Report to Congress it is stated:

> Competition is needed in the aluminum industry for reasons of national security and to help achieve prosperity. Monopoly was a burden on war production. Expansion was hampered by the fact that there was only one experienced company in this strategic industry on which our airpower depended.
>
> Multiple sources of supply are needed to develop fully the future market for aluminum. The possibilities are vast. Passenger automobiles can use 500 pounds per car effectively if supply and prices are on a competitive basis. The railroads, on the verge of a tremendous replacement program, can use large tonnages

in lightweight equipment. But all the big industrial consumers demand multiple sources of supply. The automotive industry is particularly insistent because thirty years ago it was forced to abandon its heavy use of aluminum when Alcoa raised the price from 19¢ to 33¢ within an eight months' period. The potential demand for aluminum will not crystallize into actual orders until the buyers are assured of competitive conditions. Until then they will sit by and wait, making no commitments."

* * *

"These steps should, therefore, be taken promptly:

1. In its disposal of property in this industry, the Surplus Property Board should be guided by the necessity of creating competition in the production of aluminum;

2. A complete survey ought to be made of all available bauxite reserves in this country, especially those held by Alcoa and other large companies;

3. Engineering studies should be carried on to determine power costs at various DPC producing plants and the possibilities of relocation of various plants and to determine the feasibility of cutting down the size of the larger DPC plants.

In the text of this report the conclusion is advanced that "the shortest and surest road to competition" is the subdivision of Alcoa into a few independent companies, in accordance with the Federal Court decision of March 12, 1945. There can be no doubt that if such a reorganization were undertaken there would be, as a result, more than sufficient inducement and incentive for independent operators, particularly in the West, to enter production and to strive for the cultivation of new markets. Even if this should eventually be done, however, an immense, delicate, and rather long process would be entailed. Pending the possibility of such a step potential independent producers can still be encouraged by the formulation of feasible designs for competition.

An especially helpful precedent from the standpoint of competition was established by the patent agreement negotiated between the Surplus Property Administration and Alcoa. Under this arrangement the Reconstruction Finance Corporation received free use of the Alcoa patents covering production of alumina from bauxite. The Reconstruction Finance Corporation is entitled under the agreement to sublicense these patents to any company leasing Government-owned plants. In addition to clearing this particular obstacle from the path of future competition, the agreement contributed substantially to the lease of the Government plants at Hurricane Creek, Arkansas, and Jones Mill, Arkansas, on a straight commercial basis without Government subsidy to the independent producer.

Such circumstances represent an open invitation to Western business to apply initiative to the task, because in the final analysis it is not what Government alone may or may not do but rather what free enterprise actively does that will carry the field for competition or abdicate to monopoly. The latent market for aluminum is tremendous. The multiple use of light metals which the war enhanced so notably has only opened the door to full peacetime exploitation of aluminum products. Western enterprise has a special opportunity to show that in the era of light metals a Western aluminum industry can thrive. More jobs for Western workers in aluminum mean more customers for all other Western products. More customers for all industries equal greater demand for aluminum. That is the way enterprise operates when competition turns the wheels.

CHAPTER V

The New Frontier of Technology

THE REVOLUTION in technology which is in progress can open brilliant prospects for the West. The inventions and discoveries which have come out of the war have given us manifold opportunities for adding to the array of goods and services which American industry can place on the market. New raw materials, new processes of manufacture and entirely new fields of production have been explored. New electrical equipment for the home, whole fields opened by radar, television, plastics, synthetic textiles, and new structural and building materials suggest some of the possibilities. Every industry and every type of service will be affected for the better by the more efficient techniques which have been tried out during the war.

It is readily appreciated that as yet only a small beginning has been made in this direction and that immense and intriguing advances will continue to be made. What these advances can mean in terms of opportunity for investment by Western capital, enterprise by Western businessmen, and employment for Western workers is indicated only in part by war activity in the West. Capital invested in housing, for example, creates demand for materials, electrical appliances, metal products, lumber, cement, glass, power, and ultimately for such things as furniture and textiles. As communities grow from houses, new services are in demand, new markets are formed, and new employment is opened. What is true of housing, or shipping, or aircraft is true also of investment in steel, or aluminum, or chemical factories. One enterprise spurs others, and every new market multiplies the range for employment of both capital and labor. Freedom for initiative in such fields is at a maximum in the West and will be at a maximum for years to come.

In this regard it is particularly important that as far as possible every effort be made to prevent the new technology from becoming the private reserve of monopoly groups. We know what the effects of the domination of research and technology by cartel interests have been in the past. We must face the fact that a repetition of the restriction and suppression of invention by secret agreements among industrial giants in this country and abroad or by the shortsighted action of monopolists who fear competition and who seek to protect vested position by preventing the appearance of rival producers or the introduction of improved processes would be fatal to Western industrial progress.

These assertions are given concrete form and substance if we consider the new chemical industries in the West. As in so many other fields, the existing chemical industries in this area have been greatly enlarged to meet war needs and many new chemical facilities have been established. All of us are aware, in general, of the ways in which chemical discovery is enlarging the industrial horizon. Even in a period in which all branches of technology are in a process of rapid and dynamic change, it is possible to describe this era as the age of synthetic chemistry. Literally hundreds of new chemical products have come on to the market within the last decade, and during the war chemical production reached unprecedented levels.

There is keen appreciation among Westerners of the almost unlimited scope for enterprise in chemistry. For example, Senator O'Mahoney of Wyoming in his report on postwar economic policy, stated in clarion words:

> Every observer of the industrial and economic scene is aware of the fact that one of the broadest opportunities for development in the future lies in the field of chemistry. It is not too much to say that the new frontier is in that field. When, after the Civil War, our people were seeking new outlets for their abilities and their energies, they had the vast undeveloped West to which to turn. Science and invention have opened to our gaze new visions which far exceed anything that the pioneers of seventy-five and one hundred years ago saw, but whereas the West was opened for settlement and development by every ambitious individual, that is to say, by the people in the exercise of their individual capacities, the new empires of science are already under concentrated control by reason of an archaic patent system as well as by fiscal management.
>
> . . . This is the field, not only of TNT and smokeless powder, it is the field of plastics, nylon, rayon, cellulose, alcohol, phenol, and a thousand other substances which will be the raw materials of the future.

It took almost 100 years for a few great mining corporations and industrial organizations to gain control of the mineral resources of the country. Today its chemical resources are under even tighter control as we approach the plateau from which the promised land of the future is visible.

Let no one imagine, therefore, that this is merely a question of free enterprise against Government control. It is also a question of free enterprise against monopolistic control.[1]

A typical example may be cited which will indicate why chemical industries can be especially significant in Western development, at the same time indicating the character of the impediments to their growth. In one Western state, Kansas, there is a nitrogen plant. It cost thirty million dollars ($30,000,000) and it turned out thousands of tons of nitrogen to be used in war explosives.

Now that the war is over this plant is no longer producing explosives. Although the operating company has leased the plant in the interim on a contingent basis, a choice must ultimately be made either of closing or of attempting to make nitrogen or nitrogen fertilizer. With half a chance this particular plant and two or three similar plants in the West and South would be able to make all the nitrogen which farmers would need within a radius of a thousand miles. Even more to the point, they would be able to make and sell nitrogen much more cheaply than the older plants in the East.

The basic raw materials for synthetic nitrogen

[1]"Postwar Economic Policy and Planning," Report of Hon. Joseph C. O'Mahoney, U. S. Senator from Wyoming to the Special Committee on Postwar Economic Policy and Planning, pp. 7-8, Senate Document No. 106, 78th Congress, 1st Session.

operations are hydrocarbons in various forms. The older plants of the East obtained hydrocarbons from coal gas while the newer Western plants obtained them from much cheaper natural gas. In addition to having cheaper sources of raw material, the Western plants seem to have developed an efficiency of manufacture which has astonished the established Eastern producers. When production began, Eastern advisers from older plants said, "You can't do this or that and you must do it the other way." Disregarding precedent and the advice of established manufacturers the Western management went ahead and placed the plant in operation. Almost from the outset it exceeded its estimated capacity production. The plant in Kansas turned out nitrogen products at a cost so low that it has caused much consternation among the Eastern monopoly interests. They do not yet believe the cost figures which Western plants are able to show. As one Western executive said in discussing his experience during the war, "We were not handicapped by a generation of tradition as to how nitrogen should not be made, so we went ahead and made it."

Conversion of this plant from manufacture of nitrogen for explosives to nitrogen fertilizers for both mixing and soil top dressing would represent a signal achievement to Mid-Western agriculture. The present management of the nitrogen plant in Kansas contemplates conversion from manufacture of nitrogen for explosives to nitrogen fertilizers for both mixing and soil top dressing. Even with the technical and cost advantages which it possesses, however, audacity and money will be required for a successful venture. The leaders in the nitrogen field in the United States include some of the greatest corporations in the country, such as du Pont and Allied Chemical and Dye. Such formidable opponents will not surrender the nitrogen market without a struggle. They have a dominant position in the industry and they are equipped with tremendous funds to fight a competitive battle.

It appears, moreover, that the older concerns have basic patent rights substantially covering the field of nitrogen manufacture. The ramifications which are involved in the patent question are indicated by a survey which the Kansas concern made in connection with its bid for the plant. They discovered that some 1800 patents would have to be taken into consideration. Many of these patents reach back not only to American companies but to the great chemical combines of Europe. Thus the Standard Oil Company of New Jersey controls in one way or another hundreds of patents on hydrocarbons which might be involved when natural gas is used as raw material for nitrogen production. The du Pont Company has hundreds more of patents on the so-called chemical process. The Barrett Company and several others have patent interests in various related processes.

During the war patents were cleared through the War Department. Now that the war is over the patent situation as it affects civilian operations is almost completely clouded. Whether the Kansas company will be able to operate under reasonable licenses or whether it will be unable to withstand the possibility of protracted patent litigation is a serious question.

The West possesses many other chemical industries, some old and some new. There is, for instance, an alcohol plant in Omaha which was built at a cost of nearly six million dollars ($6,000,000) to make alcohol from the grains and other farm products of the region. Why should its closing be permanent? Again, in Denver, the Rocky Mountain Arsenal owned by the Government produced a number of chemicals, among which probably the most important was chlorine. The arsenal had an operating capacity of 30,000 tons per year for this product alone.

Quite clearly the West has many sources of raw materials other than hydrocarbons available for a strong and competitive chemical industry. We may recognize that new industries and new products would flow in great numbers from a competitive Western chemical industry, but at the same time the obstacles are also numerous and complex. We know that the chemical industry in the past, both in this country and in the foreign market, has been thoroughly cartelized. We know also that every major branch of chemical production has been dominated in one way or another by huge patent pools and patent cartels. It would be difficult, if not impossible, to forecast at this time exactly what situations will be encountered by Western chemical producers with respect to their patent positions. To the extent that major abuses of patents can be eliminated and to the degree that new chemical technology can be freed from domination by monopoly groups it should become possible and attractive for Western producers to enter the field. In this regard it may be said that the antitrust actions by the Government within recent years have done much to remove the worst types of abuse by which monopoly seeks to control technological change. Given the alertness and active support of regional industry, the development of chemical production in the West has exceptionally favorable chances to keep pace with its ever-widening possibilities.

CHAPTER VI

Land and People

THE WEST has tremendous resources. It is this setting, plus the combination of war industries and people aroused to the problem of industrial progress which make possible an economic renaissance in the West.

It is always somewhat astounding to contemplate this region. In terms of space the West is an empire within itself. Some of the states are larger than entire sections of the East. Many Western States are larger than whole nations of Europe. Out of a total area of some 3,000,000 square miles for the country, the fifteen Western States have an area of 1,500,000 square miles. Such figures, of course, have more definite meaning to one who travels over the country. For instance, from Omaha to San Francisco it is nearly 1800 miles; from Omaha to Scottsbluff, both of which are in the State of Nebraska, it is 430 miles, almost as far as from Washington to Boston. Nebraska alone exceeds all of New England in size. California alone is as large as New England and the Middle Atlantic States together.

The resources of the West correspond to its dimensions. The diversity and extent of natural wealth in this section make it the great reservoir of the nation for many of the essential materials of American industry. Any one of the groups of resources would provide adequate subject matter for a series of learned dissertations. We must content ourselves, however, with a cursory survey of some of the more important and strategic materials.

To begin with, the agricultural products of the West range from fruits and vegetables to sheep and cattle. They provide a large part of our national sustenance. In the cattle industry the dominance of the West is undisputed. In 1942 the West had 35% of the total value of cattle in the United States; 58% of the sheep and wool; 70% of the wheat; 72% of the sugar beets.

The agricultural fertility of the West is not news, but it is still impressive that out of a total wheat crop in 1942 valued at more than one billion dollars ($1,000,000,000) nearly 70% was produced in the fifteen Western States. Other Western grains also run to large figures whether we speak of corn or oats or barley or rye. Taken together these figures leave no room for dispute that the great Western valley is indeed the national granary.[1]

There are many other important products of Western agriculture. One of these is sugar beets. In 1942 some fifty-seven million dollars ($57,000,000) worth of sugar beets were produced in the Western States or 72% of the national total. They had a value of one hundred thirty-two million dol-

[1]The value of the more important agricultural products of the West will be found in Table II, on Page 153 in the Appendix.

lars ($132,000,000) when reduced to beet sugar. Even in agricultural commodities, however, we encounter evidences of the historic colonial policy by which Western products are controlled by Eastern interests. In the case of beet sugar, the highest price in the entire country is charged at the factory door in Colorado. This comes about because sugar is sold on a basing point price system similar to the one already met in the steel industry. The coastal refineries of the East, the West and the South fix the base prices of beet sugar. The price at the point of delivery inland increases in exact proportion to the freight rates from the seaboard, even though the beet sugar of the West may move only a few miles to the grocery store. Such a pricing system would be logical in *Alice in Wonderland*. In our national economy, however, it is completely upside down.

Closely related to the products which have been mentioned are the fruits and vegetables of the West. Without undertaking a statistical survey we may simply note in passing that many types of fruits, such as pears, plums and prunes, are primarily Western in origin. A major part of the American supply of edible nuts, such as almonds, filberts and walnuts, comes entirely from the Pacific Coast States. Lemons, lettuce, oranges, peaches, grapes and apples from the Western farm areas contribute to the diet of the entire nation. With more rapid and cheaper means of transportation, including air transport, the market for Western fruits and vegetables can be greatly expanded. Thousands of farmers would be able to supply many thousands more of eager consumers if fast air cargo brought the products of Western agriculture in quantities large enough to make their prices within the reach of the average purchaser.

Among the natural resources of the West the lumber and timber supply occupy a position of major importance. The fifteen Western States produce more than half of the total output of soft woods. In 1940 this output was valued at more than three hundred sixteen million dollars ($316,000,000), out of a total lumber production including both hard and soft woods of five hundred sixty million dollars ($560,000,000). Such woods as Douglas fir, and Ponderosa pine are particularly prominent in the Western lumber industry. When translated into board feet, the available timber resources must be calculated in astronomical figures. For example some 12-15,000,000,000 feet of timber are produced annually in the West.

In the long run the total stand of timber in the West is more important than figures of annual production. In 1938 the estimated stand of Western soft woods large enough to be used for timber was approximately 1,216,000,000,000 board feet. In other words, if we assume an annual production of about 14,000,000,000 board feet, Western forests still contain about one hundred years' supply of timber. With reasonable care and allowing for both normal growth and normal cutting there should be an indefinite, almost perpetual supply of soft woods in the West capable of providing for the national market for generations.[2]

Farmers in the West, as elsewhere, have been at grips with many difficult situations in the past. Some

[2]A statistical breakdown of available timber by type, price and value will be found in Table III, page 154 in the Appendix.

of these difficulties are the result of long-run changes in the position of agriculture in our economy, while others are the product of emergency conditions. The States, the Federal Government, and the farmers themselves, in their cooperatives, have been engaged for many years in formulating and applying policies to deal with the long trends and special circumstances which must be met. These programs are so broad in scope and so complex in detail that their review would go far beyond the limits of this study.

Certain factors affecting the future of western agriculture, however, are in the direct line of our inquiry. A free society cannot be indifferent to the welfare of the farms and forests which sustain life, or to the well-being of the people who raise crops and cattle for all consumers. It is widely understood that the conservation of agricultural and forest resources, and the maintenance of range land and soil fertility are matters of national concern. The promotion, as far as possible, of the economic effectiveness of family-size farms is conceded to be both socially and economically desirable.

Agricultural research, scientific forestry, irrigation, and advances in chemistry can be increasingly available to help agriculture to further these aims. The conservation of resources is accompanied by the production of better crops. New methods of packing and refrigeration, together with faster, cheaper transport, will do much to extend the market for agricultural products, cut down margins of loss in crop value, and increase farm buying power.

It is not so readily appreciated that the farmer is peculiarly the victim of monopoly conditions in other branches of the economy. Western agricultural industries stand to gain permanent benefits as basic regional disadvantages are removed, and as resources are better utilized. But both as producers and consumers, farmers will share in the broader economic development of the West as markets are freed from monopoly practices.

It cannot be too strongly stated that any permanent solution of the problems of farmers depends upon eliminating monopoly practices in industry generally. When industrial output is governed by the scarcity philosophy of monopoly, agricultural raw materials and products are devalued, not by competition, but by a market in which the ratios of exchange are weighted against them. When prices of industrial products are held rigid by monopoly agreement, agricultural prices must bear the brunt of a decline in demand. Only when competitive conditions prevail in industry will an equitable market relationship make it possible to work for lasting adjustments.

In the period before the war, for instance, farmers had to buy fertilizers at monopoly prices because international cartels controlled nitrogen, phosphates, and potash. Farm machinery and equipment have been frequent subjects of monopoly practices and cartel arrangements. Independent farmers have found time and again that while they had to sell their products on a highly competitive basis, the system of distribution was itself monopolistically controlled.

Illustrations of such conditions have been frequently encountered in antitrust cases. For example, meat packers had devised the system of market-sharing which divided livestock receipts from cattle, hogs, calves, and sheep, in central markets. Fixed percentages of the market were allotted among the buyers, with no competitive bidding on prices. Sometimes the buyers took turns in making offers; at other times dice were rolled to determine who would do the purchasing. All prices offered were agreed on in advance.

Other such cases involved large fruit and vegetable processors and packers who entered into contracts with growers which limited acreage, and allocated growers among the processors. The processors fixed by agreement the prices which growers were to receive.

Under such restraints the farmer sells less, and receives less, while the consumer pays higher prices and therefore is unable to buy as much as he would at lower prices. Larger incomes for farmers, lower prices for the necessities they must have from industry, and better diets for consumers are part of a single purpose. To agriculture, the successful linking of this economic chain is the important task of tomorrow.

One cannot discuss the resources of the West without taking into account its most important asset, Westerners themselves. It has already been mentioned that during the war years the migration of workers, the movement of troops and the great increase in travel which accompanied the war effort have churned and regrouped Western population. Nevertheless, with respect to population, as in so many other ways, the West is still a frontier. In fact, it may be said that population is one of the principal question marks of the Western future.

Although the fifteen Western States contain 50%

of the land area of the country, in 1940 they had only 14% of the national population. Over much of this area, population trends indicate that growth has come to a halt and in some cases has begun to decline. Any worthwhile remedy for Western problems must therefore give serious consideration to the population problem.

Over the general area it is noticeable that there are both under-population and very uneven distribution. During the war people have crowded into war centers, so that some metropolitan areas on the Pacific Coast increased more than 50% in population within four or five years. The major cities of California, Oregon and Washington are notoriously overcrowded. Around the San Francisco Bay and around Los Angeles hundreds of thousands of people moved in to provide labor for the war plants. From April, 1940, to November, 1943, the civilian population of California increased by about 15%; that of Washington increased about 11%; that of Oregon about 8%.

In the main, the population growth of the Coast attributable to the demands of war occurred largely at the expense of other Western states. During the period from 1940 to 1943 the civilian population of Nebraska declined some 11%; North and South Dakota lost 15%; and Montana lost 16%. These great shifts of people from the Plains and Mountains to the Coast are symptoms of a great economic disturbance. If they are not compensated, they represent a distinct threat to the development of the area east of the Rocky Mountains. It is clear from an examination of special reports made by the Bureau of the Census that this division of population was accelerated during the war, so that in the fifteen states under consideration, almost every state east of the Mountains shows a decline, while every state west of the Mountains shows a relative increase.[3]

The West needs people if it is to have large industries. It needs large industries if it is to attract and hold an adequate population. Some idea of the room for growth in this respect is given by the opinion of experts in such matters that a total of 50,000,000 people will be needed within the next half century for the optimum development of Western resources. In other words, the West needs symmetry and growth in population as well as industrial expansion if its capacities are to be translated into economic reality. During the period from 1900 to 1940 the population of the West increased from 7,350,000 to 18,285,000. This represents a gain of roughly 150% but it is not enough. It will require prolonged and determined effort on the part of those most vitally concerned in the future of the West to capitalize the initial impetus which the war has provided, so that in time the West may have enough people to fulfill its needs.

Without people in sufficient numbers, neither industry nor agriculture can grow. Men and women with vision and courage won the old West. Men and women with the desire and ability to work, to engage in enterprise, and to build will be needed if the land is to flourish. There is a new West to be won.

[3]For estimated change in civilian population in the Western States during the War see Table IV, p. 154 of the Appendix.

CHAPTER VII

Mineral and Energy Resources

FOR ALMOST a century the West has been a storehouse of America's mineral and energy resources. When early settlers first struck out into the relatively unknown territory of the West they were primarily seeking land. As they progressed they looked upon the rolling grasslands, the mountains, the deserts, the plateaus, and the great rivers of the region. They settled in the valleys, the coastal areas and the fertile table lands. It was the discovery of gold, silver, and other minerals, however, that started the biggest wave of migrants. The prospector and his burro in search of the new "strike" ultimately unearthed apparently inexhaustible supplies of wealth. At first there was some reckless exploitation of the most accessible and richest lodes, leaving only "ghost towns" to mark their sites. But normal commercial demands have also taken their toll. A world at war has an insatiable appetite for minerals, and unavoidable depletion has occurred in the case of some of the better-known deposits. Yet, though its metals and fuels have been chewed up at a staggering rate in the past fifty years, there are few areas anywhere which can match the mineral reserves of the West.

Minerals such as gold, silver, copper and lead are still primarily the products of the West. Industrially necessary ores and strategic metals such as tungsten, molybdenum, vanadium, manganese and zinc are all found here. Less well known but equally vital minerals such as chrome, mercury and specialized ores have also been located and exploited. Even now new types of minerals are being discovered in the West. One class of Western ores may become especially important in the future. These are the radioactive ores scattered throughout the West which have been or may be used in the development of atomic energy and power. In the long future, these substances may rank among the most important raw materials in the world.

Some of the mineral resources which are included in the total production of the West merit more than mention, not only because of their intrinsic value but because they have come to be the basis of great industries reflecting the forces of economic concentration as well as geographic concentration which account so largely for the disadvantages under which Western industry has developed. Thus copper has been one of the principal mineral products of the West for two generations. Copper overshadows all other Western metals in value. Its annual production is valued at approximately two hundred sixty-seven million dollars ($267,000,000) per year. Arizona, as the chief producing state, yielded one hundred and five million dollars ($105,000,000) worth of copper in 1933; Utah ranked next with eighty-four million dollars ($84,000,000); Montana produced thirty-five million dollars ($35,000,000) worth of copper; and New Mexico produced about twenty million dollars ($20,000,000) worth. The total copper produced by the fifteen Western States represents about 95% of the value of production for the country as a whole.

Copper is probably the world's oldest metal. Archeologists believe that its use goes back before the dawn of history, and they speak of the Bronze Age, when tools and weapons were made of an alloy of tin and copper, as the period in which men first learned to employ metals instead of primitive stone implements. Although copper was used by the Indians long before Columbus discovered the New World, the rise of the American copper industry to world importance really began in the Seventies and Eighties of the last century.

Today, the gold and silver which attracted pioneers are by-products of copper. The copper production of Arizona, Montana, Utah, and other states began at a time when electricity was being introduced into industry. Since that time, the oldest metal has been principally employed in the most modern of industries, for electric cables, coils, transmission lines, and similar equipment. Much copper goes into automobiles and machinery of all types, as well as into more humble uses, such as the indispensable penny. In national defense, copper is among the most essential of all materials—in fact, it is comparable to steel and aluminum in military importance.

The figures of copper production, and the variety

of its uses are significant in themselves. More significant in economic terms, however, is the fact that copper production is largely controlled by three great corporations. These companies, Kennecott, Anaconda and Phelps Dodge, together control about 85% of all copper produced in this country. This concentration of control is the product of many years of expansion, at times gradual and at times very rapid. In 1920 the Big Three copper companies controlled slightly more than 25% of the output. In 1930 they controlled about 40%. By 1940 the ownership of the Big Three encompassed nearly 80% of the copper produced and during the years of the war this percentage has increased to about 85%. In addition to domestic sources, two of the Big Three companies owned the copper mines of Chile, the principal source of imports. With this addition it may be conservatively estimated that the three companies supply 90% of all copper consumed in the United States.

An analysis of the division of control among the Big Three shows that Kennecott is the major figure in the industry. In 1920 Kennecott held about 4% of the total production and Phelps Dodge about 5.6%. By 1930 Kennecott had increased its percentage to 13% and Anaconda held about 19%. In this same period, Phelps Dodge was still relatively small, holding about 8%. A decade later in 1940 Kennecott had forged to the front in a decisive manner by controlling more than 40% of the total national production. In the same year Anaconda accounted for 20% and Phelps Dodge for 18%. During the peak of war production in 1943 Kennecott had 43% of the national total, Anaconda 19%, and Phelps Dodge something over 22%.[1]

It is evident that with this degree of concentration of control over the great mineral industry, price competition will inevitably be held to a minimum for the elementary reason that it does not pay any one of the companies to cut prices. Any price reduction by one company is instantly met by its fellows. Such a condition, which is often called monopolistic competition, produces much the same results from the standpoint of the market as if the entire industry were controlled by a single concern. In these circumstances and in the absence of extreme depression, prices tend to move in only one direction, that is, upward. From this standpoint any question of price understandings or gentlemen's agreements among the big copper companies becomes largely academic because prices will "behave" without the necessity of any formal commitments.

Not only do the Big Three companies dominate the production of the metal but they are also the principal fabricators of copper products. Together with the American Smelting and Refining Company, the Big Three manufacture most of the copper sheets, rods, wire castings, forgings, bars, extrusions and similar items. It is especially significant that for the most part copper products are not fabricated in the West where the copper is produced and where many of the finished articles are consumed. What we find instead is a repetition of the historic policy of trans-shipment. Copper from Western mines is hauled thousands of miles across the country at com-

[1]The percentage control of mine production of copper in the United States is shown in Table V, p. 155 in the Appendix.

paratively high freight rates, fabricated into finished products and then shipped back across the country for such consumption as may be found at the high prices resulting from such circumstances.

The control of copper by a few companies is not limited to the United States. Between the wars a world copper cartel operated for various periods under several successive names. The methods of control took various forms. Immediately after the close of the First World War a copper export association was formed which earmarked domestic surplus for export and doled the surplus out over several years as the market would accept it. In the late 1920's the general breakdown of the market wrecked this association. A company was then formed called Copper Exporters which had two branches, one operating in New York and the other in Brussels, Belgium. The principal function of this company operating through two cities was to fix the price of copper in the world market. At about the same time, in 1930, the Copper Institute was established in the United States and reached an agreement with foreign producers.

In 1930 it was agreed to reduce the production of copper all over the world by 20% (about 288,000 tons per year). Twenty-one domestic and foreign companies subscribed to this agreement, including the Chilean mines of Anaconda and Kennecott, and the Katanga in Africa. Like its predecessors, the Copper Institute did not survive the depression of the early 1930's, but in 1935 the foreign production agreement was renewed as it applied to the Western Hemisphere with particular respect to Chile and

Mexico. This time it was agreed to curtail production by amounts ranging up to 30 and 40%.

From the standpoint of our national economy the control of copper and copper products presents a typical big business pattern and a typical division of interests between the East and the West. Three or four companies obtain the ore from the West, refine it, haul it many miles to Eastern mills, fabricate it and ship it back again. If the West had fabricating plants and if there were some price competition in copper products, the whole United States would get copper at a lower price. Even without increased price competition, which is improbable when three or four companies control the bulk of production, the removal of the cost of multiple freight hauls would normally result in lower delivered prices.

A few words should be said concerning the alloy metals found in the West, particularly with reference to the ferro-alloys. The ferro-alloy industry of the United States is comparatively large and of comparatively recent origin, since its growth has occurred principally during the past twenty-five years. In 1943 the total value of production of these alloys was more than two hundred and seventy million dollars ($270,000,000). Ferromanganese was first on the list with a value of ninety-three million five hundred thousand dollars ($93,500,000). Ferrosilicon and ferrochrome ranked next, each having a value of about forty-seven million dollars ($47,-000,000). Ferromolybdenum and its compounds were valued at about thirty-one million dollars ($31,-000,000) and ferrovanadium at about twelve million dollars ($12,000,000). The entire field, therefore, ranks as one of the large industries of the country.

The production and sale of ferro-alloys are even more tightly controlled than they are in the copper industry. As a rule, two companies and at most three companies produce the bulk of each one of the important alloys. For example, two companies account for the entire production of ferrovanadium. Similarly, two companies produce more than 99% of the ferromolybdenum. The same is true of ferrotungsten. Although there are half a dozen producers of ferrochrome, one company accounts for 75% of the total output. In ferrotitanium there is one large producer and two or three much smaller concerns. In the fields of the more complex alloys it is found more often than not that a single company is responsible for our entire domestic production.

Although two or three companies ordinarily dominate each branch of ferro-alloy production, it should of course be understood that they are not always the same group. Six companies produce several different alloys in various proportions. The largest in the field is the Electro Metallurgical Corporation, which makes ferrovanadium, molybdenum, tungsten, chrome, titanium, boron and several other types. The Molybdenum Corporation of America also produces a number of the ferro-alloys.

It has been pointed out in the discussion of copper that when the control of an industry is highly concentrated among a relatively few producers, price competition is reduced to a minimum. This principle is again borne out in the field of ferro-alloys. With the two companies mentioned above controlling practically all the production of the more important alloys, there is little chance for price competition to emerge. This is particularly true in this field because the volume of sales does not fluctuate so much with the price of the alloys themselves as with a totally independent factor: the production of steel in which the alloys are used. As a consequence, the two or three principal producers of each type of alloy are in a position to charge according to the ancient dictum, "what the traffic will bear." Although, in general, these alloys do not constitute an important part of the cost of producing ordinary steel, they do become a sizeable factor in the case of special steels. From the standpoint of the consumer the high prices of these alloys are simply another item of cost which they must pay when they purchase steel products.

Cartelization is also manifest in the ferro-alloy industry. The producers of some of the ferro-alloys participate in international cartels so that in addition to control of the domestic market, their position is fortified in the world market. In the case of molybdenum, for instance, the producers of this metal entered into an agreement with the international ferromolybdenum convention to which producers in Germany, Great Britain and France also adhered. Although the Colorado mines produced most of the world's molybdenum, some quantities are found in half a dozen countries and there are many companies abroad buying molybdenum concentrates and manufacturing ferromolybdenum for the steel industry.

The cartel divided the world into five parts. The American companies were given North and South America, China, Japan and Russia for their markets. The French companies were allotted French territory and the colonies and protectorates of

France scattered around the world. The German company was given the German Reich and the English interests received the United Kingdom and Ireland.

In general, the contract provided that molybdenum would not be sold in any form for the manufacture of iron and steel by any company in the exclusive territory of another nor in the joint territory of the group except under certain specified conditions. In return, it was understood that foreign producers would not attempt to invade the American market.

In 1941 the Department of Justice instituted action against this cartel arrangement and a decree was obtained in 1942 cancelling the agreement and forbidding further a participation in the cartel by the American companies. Even though legal relief was obtained, however, it should be borne in mind that where so few companies control production the behavior of price may be restricted without the necessity of formal understanding simply because the market is closed.

The products and industries which have been mentioned by no means exhaust the list of important Western minerals. The West produces 90% of the annual output of gold. Sixty per cent of the national total of zinc production comes from the West. In 1943 the Western States had a zinc output valued at eighty-two million dollars ($82,000,000).[2] Lead production in the West is valued at about thirty-six

[2]Zinc production is geographically well distributed. Idaho had about nineteen million dollars ($19,000,000) worth, New Mexico $13,000,000, Kansas $12,300,000, Utah $10,000,000, and Colorado $9,500,000.

million dollars ($36,000,000) annually or nearly 60% of the national total. In the case of silver the West produces more than 99% of the total output.[3]

To this list of mineral resources may be added some items of significance to the farmers. In 1943 potash for fertilizer produced in New Mexico was valued at twenty-two million dollars ($22,000,000) or nearly 85% of the total domestic supply. In this connection it should be recalled that in pre-war years more than 50% of the potash supply was imported. In future years, however, imports of potash will probably be relatively low because of the large volume and low cost of domestic production in the West. Equally interesting, although not so important at the present time, is the possibility of increased production of phosphates in the West if the mines in Idaho, Montana and Utah can compete with those in Florida and Tennessee.

If we add to this roster of mineral wealth the vast energy resources which the West possesses in coal, water power, oil and natural gas, it is evident that only in our imaginations can we comprehend more than a fragment of the total which is present. There is enough coal in the West alone to supply the demands of the United States at current rates of consumption for thousands of years. The Bureau of Mines estimates that total coal reserves are 2,225,000,000,000 tons of bituminous and sub-bituminous grades. Of this astronomical figure 50% is located in six of the public land states of the West.[4]

[3]The value of the more important mineral products of the West will be found in Table VI, page 156 in the Appendix.
[4]The coal resources in the public land states will be found in Table VII, page 158 in the Appendix.

The prodigious size of coal reserves have more meaning when we interpret them to indicate that the Plains States and the Mountain States probably have more coal than we shall ever use in the foreseeable future. It is scarcely necessary to allude to the figures of petroleum reserves or to the alarming rate at which these reserves are being depleted. It may be pointed out, however, that even at this experimental stage of development it is possible to produce synthetic petroleum and other hydrocarbons from coal at a price of 10¢ or 12¢ per gallon. In the course of time it seems a safe guess that gasoline will be produced from coal at about the same price as that at which gasoline now comes from the petroleum refinery, or about 5¢ per gallon. After our petroleum is gone, if it ever does go, we should be able to run our automobiles for generations on the gasoline from coal or from the oil shales of Colorado and Utah. It is estimated that these sources would yield about 75,000,000,000 barrels of fuel. Over that many years, however, it may be just as likely that we shall run automobiles on atomic energy.

In addition to coal reserves, the water power resources of the West will become increasingly important. The rivers of the Mountain States already produce enormous quantities of electric power. The Federal Power Commission estimates that the Pacific and Mountain Coast States have undeveloped water power resources of some 21,000,000 kilowatts. The existing water power stations now turn out about 4,500,000 kilowatts. There is, therefore, still a long way to go before this Western potential power is fully exploited. This water power can produce economic miracles if it is utilized to provide the basis for new, vigorous industrial areas in which enterprise is turned loose.

Last but not least, the petroleum produced in the West leads all other commodities in terms of value. In 1943 the fifteen Western States produced more than five hundred million dollars ($500,000,000) worth of petroleum or nearly 30% of the total production of this country. Of this Western total, more than three hundred million dollars ($300,000,000) came from California while Kansas accounted for a share valued at one hundred thirty million dollars ($130,000,000).

It has been necessary throughout this chapter to cite long figures. On paper these figures are dry statistics. It should be realized, however, that they represent only a slight glimpse of the riches of the West, riches so great that no individual could ever adequately explore them all. What these figures tell us is that the West, in terms of potential growth, is still a frontier. The question is whether this frontier will ever be developed to its fullest extent in such a way that Western enterprise, Western capital and Western labor participate directly in the benefits.

CHAPTER VIII

The War Industries of the West

WHEN WE come to consider the vast quantity of war supplies which the West produced it is apparent that the war industries of the West have shown that they can more than keep pace with other sections of the country. The growth of various types of industry in the Western States during the war has already been discussed but it is worthwhile to fill in some specific details.

The totals of war supplies, not including the construction of the war plants themselves, produced by the fifteen Western States are almost unbelievable. In round numbers the war contracts for these fifteen states through April, 1945, amounted to twenty-nine billion dollars ($29,000,000,000). This represents an enormous amount of commodities—ships, airplanes, food, mineral products, chemicals, ammunition and a thousand and one other items of which we rarely hear in times of peace. These twenty-nine billions of war contracts are more than five times the total value for all manufactured products in the West in the year 1939. For the average war year, war supplies alone were produced on a scale 50% more than civilian manufacture before the war.

It is true that heavy war production was concentrated in several of the Western States. California, for example, had nearly eighteen billion dollars ($18,000,000,000) of the twenty-nine billion total; Washington had four billion five hundred fifty million ($4,550,000,000) and Oregon had nearly one billion seven hundred ninety million ($1,790,000,000) of the supply contracts for the whole period.

The inland states, however, did their share. Kansas, for example, had more than three billion dollars ($3,000,000,000) worth of the supply contracts as compared with manufacturing production in 1939 of about four hundred sixty-five million dollars ($465,-000,000). Nebraska had war supply contracts valued at nine hundred twenty-seven million dollars ($927,-000,000); Colorado had three hundred eighty-four million dollars ($384,000,000); and Wyoming had more than sixty-five million dollars ($65,000,000).

On a relative basis the Western States showed a gain slightly above the country as a whole in war supply contracts as compared with total prewar manufacturing. In 1939 the fifteen Western States produced 10% of the value of manufactures for the country whereas they had 15% of the war supply contracts.[1]

One difficulty with the enormous war expansion of the West from the standpoint of conversion is

[1]A detailed analysis of war contracts by states as compared with prewar manufacturing is shown in Table VIII, p. 158 in the Appendix.

that it is somewhat too highly concentrated geographically to be well located for the manufacture of civilian products. Even aside from the concentration in particular states, one of the most noticeable features of Western war industries is that they are centered about relatively small areas within the states. Thus California has war plants valued at one billion four hundred fifty million dollars ($1,450,000,000), or about 45% of the Western total, but most of these are found in the Los Angeles and San Francisco areas. Los Angeles alone has some eight hundred million dollars ($800,000,000) worth of facilities while San Francisco has five hundred million dollars ($500,000,000) worth.

The distribution of war facilities in the other Western states presents much the same picture. It is understandable, of course, that war plants were located at sites which made possible the most rapid construction and operation. Time was of the essence, and it is an unavoidable consequence that some localities within states now have cases of congestion which will need to be remedied.[2]

Although decentralization and dispersion of plants are not ends in themselves, the reconversion plans of Western industry should attempt to follow the most up-to-date methods of industrial management in the selection of sites. Their chances of successful operation will be greatly aided if this is done. In the older industrial section of the East factories often "just growed" in a somewhat haphazard manner, with resulting disadvantages in long-run competitive value. The exercise of care in

[2]A further analysis of such local concentration is given in Table IX, p. 159 in the Appendix.

plant location, plus the adoption of streamlined techniques, made possible by the youthfulness of many Western plants will undoubtedly give them a strong position in open competition. Not only the enterprises concerned, but also the communities in which they are situated would then benefit from better distribution of people and opportunity.

It is interesting to examine the record of the war economy for a state like Nebraska. Although this is one of the smaller states in terms of the amount of war plants and war contracts which were allotted to it, it had a total investment in these plants of one hundred eight million dollars ($108,000,000) at the end of 1944. Out of this total the Federal Government supplied almost exactly one hundred million dollars ($100,000,000) while private industry provided the remainder. Compared to the country as a whole or to the war plant investment of some of its western neighbors the Nebraska investment is relatively small. Nevertheless, a lot of plant facilities can be built with one hundred million dollars ($100,000,000).

Although the war plants of Nebraska are fairly well scattered, the Omaha area heads the list with some forty-two million dollars ($42,000,000), a very substantial share of the total. Wahoo, 30 miles west of Omaha, has thirty million dollars ($30,000,000) worth of plants, Grand Island has more than twenty-three million dollars ($23,000,000) of war plants and Lincoln has more than seven million dollars ($7,000,000).

The Nebraska war plants produced an amazing variety of commodities. B-29 Superfortresses were made at the rate of more than fifty a month. Together with an assembly plant for B-26's some one hundred thirty-five planes a month were produced. The plants engaged in aircraft production had a value of more than twenty-two million dollars ($22,-000,000). It may be noted that in addition to the other plants there is an aircraft modification center in Omaha which cost approximately seven million dollars ($7,000,000). It seems reasonable to ask why, if Omaha can support such a large aircraft manufacturing industry in wartime, it cannot support at least some fair portion of that industry in times of peace.

Many other important wartime products were produced in the Omaha area. There is a great alcohol plant which has a capacity of fifty thousand gallons of alcohol per day, and which cost nearly six million dollars ($6,000,000). Another important project is the manufacture of steel castings. The facilities for this commodity have a capacity of nearly ten thousand tons per month and cost nearly three-quarters of a million dollars.

Tens of millions of pounds of food products were processed in Omaha. Canned meats, dried eggs, all types of cereals, sausages and lard as well as the great staples like beef and pork were turned out at rates of millions of pounds per month. One dried-egg plant alone cost well over a million dollars and produced several million pounds per year, while still other plants have capacity to produce twenty million pounds of corn flour and fifty million tons of mixed feeds. Omaha is also a principal center for creamery products.

Other cities in Nebraska have also acquired or expanded war plants of respectable size. In Lincoln, for example, there was a war plant producing a modest but important product—self-locking elastic stop nuts. This plant cost more than four million dollars ($4,000,000) and was capable of producing more than two hundred million units per month. This volume of production seems to have been some sort of record. Also in Lincoln there was a plant which cost more than one million six hundred thousand dollars ($1,600,000) producing portable telephones and accessories. Bomb fuses, self-sealing fuel tanks, and rubber tires are among other commodities which war plants in this locality produced, in addition to the operation of great bomb-loading plants.

The war supply contracts which these and other plants in Nebraska fulfilled run into much larger figures than the cost of the plants themselves. The total supply contracts in the state through April, 1945, amounted to more than nine hundred twenty-seven million dollars ($927,000,000). Of this amount seventy-five per cent was represented by aircraft and another fifteen per cent by ordnance. Further breakdown of these figures into the more specific products which make up the accumulative total during the war is not readily available, but contracts as of June 30, 1945, contained many large items which are significant because they show what the state can do.[3]

The questions which arise from this review of war industries in Nebraska indicate the scope and complexity of economic adjustment which even a single state must make in transferring its energies to

[3]The important war plants and war contracts in Nebraska are shown in Tables X and XI, pp. 160-162 of the Appendix.

peacetime production. It is not simply a matter of industry in Nebraska resuming a prewar scale of operations or taking up again exactly the same types of activity which composed its economic life before the war. We must ask not only how many of the war plants have been locked up with the cessation of war contracts; we must also ask whether if Nebraskan industry can load bombs, make fuses, and construct and operate a large alcohol plant, such creative ability cannot find peacetime outlets. It would be a serious economic error as well as a great economic loss to allow any wartime development which might conceivably be utilized for peacetime production to be closed down for want of adequate markets or lack of clear-cut reconversion policies. Unfortunately, many of the plants that led Nebraska's war effort have already shut their doors or have been reduced to skeleton proportions. In other instances, war plants have been closed and reopened as branches of Eastern concerns. It is a responsibility, as well as an opportunity, for local capital in Nebraska and other Western States to attempt such reconversion on its own behalf if the full benefits of industrialization are to be realized. Ample reserves of capital are present in the West. What is needed to transform them into industrial investment is industrial alertness and confidence in the capabilities of the region.

Like citizens throughout the country, the citizens of Nebraska have an immediate and definite interest in exerting every possible effort to salvage as much industrial capacity as they can to be used for the future economic well-being of the state. The people of Nebraska, or Wyoming, or Oregon, or any other Western State owe it to themselves, and to the nation, to seek out and pursue all ways of utilizing their human and material resources. Land, labor, and capital do not automatically produce wealth or give employment. It is initiative which combines them, and enterprise which makes them successful. What the rest of the country owes to the Western States in this effort is a guarantee that opportunities will not be foreclosed, and that the markets of the nation will be open to new industry.

CHAPTER IX

The Development of the Missouri Valley

THE MISSOURI RIVER and its tributaries form one of the great hydrographic systems of the earth. Large parts of nine states are drained by one or more of the streams within the system. Several of the states are entirely within the drainage basin. The main stream is approximately 2500 miles long and is supplemented by thousands of branches and sub-branches. From the western part of Montana and northern Wyoming the waters of half a dozen great rivers converge into the principal stream flowing through the Dakotas. Between Nebraska and Iowa the main stream is joined by the Platte River and between Kansas and Missouri by the Kaw River. Winter snows and spring rains accumulate a tremendous head of water, which if uncontrolled, sweeps the valleys for thousands of square miles. In the summer and in the autumn the rainfall is deficient and great areas are parched for want of moisture.

This river system and the territory which it drains form the boundaries of the Missouri Valley. The eastern part of the Valley is one of the principal agricultural regions of the world. It is remarkable, however, that this fabulous basin as a whole is only now being gradually appreciated. Plans are either now in process or contemplated which will, if they are realized, transform the Missouri Valley into a fertile and productive inland empire.

For two hundred years settlers from the Atlantic Coast pushed westward over the Alleghenies and through the forests of the Cumberland, the Ohio and the St. Lawrence basin. When, in the middle of the last century, they approached the western edge of the forest along a line roughly demarcated by the Mississippi River, they were hesitant to plunge into the unknown sweep of the great plains. This was a new land covered for endless miles with tall grass which could furnish none of the amenities of the forest to which they were accustomed. In clearing forests the settlers at the same time provided timber for building homes. The forests furnished the fuel and supported the wildlife from which the settlers obtained much of their food. All the necessities of life could be obtained with a reasonable amount of effort and the economy of the household was practically self-contained.

On the great plains such adjustment was not possible. The grassy slopes furnished neither material for houses nor fuel. Indeed, the grass itself because of its inflammability constituted a hazard. The absence of trees appeared to indicate the poverty of the soil and the scarcity of water was a danger not to be taken lightly. As a result of these first impressions of the plains, they were considered to be an obstacle to be hastily by-passed in the migration farther west toward more familiar timber and water lands in the foothills of the Rocky Mountains. It is safe to say that the great plains lost a full generation of settlers because of the strange and rather forbidding appearance which they presented to the eyes of the migrants.

It was not until the railroads opened up the country and barbed wire fenced it and steel plows broke its surface that the Western plain was tamed. These three factors are mentioned with some deliberation because just as the streams of the East were highways for opening the country so were the railroads across the plains and the wagon trails that branched from them the means for opening up the Middle West. Without the cheap and useful barbed wire fences, farms and ranches would have been merely a part of the great outdoors. Steel plows were the principal instruments necessary to the cultivation of tough prairie sod. It is only recently, almost within the memory of the living generation, that the Western plains have been brought under a measure of control by this combination of transport and farming.

Everyone who has lived in the West knows that it is a hard country to fight. In the first place it has one of the most volatile climates in the world. Within the space of a few hours it blows hot and cold, wet and dry. Partly this capricious weather is induced by the endless flat plains which present no obstacle to the wind and partly it results from the convergence of three great contending climatic forces. One of them is the great reservoir of cold air that moves south from the Canadian tundra on to the northern plains and at times, especially in winter, shows a cold front as far south as Texas. The second force is the maritime air from the Gulf of Mexico and the south Atlantic which sweeps up the Mississippi Valley in the springtime and awakens the West. The third force is made up of the dry winds prevalent in summer and fall which come from Mexico and Texas and form a wedge between the cold front from the north and the maritime air from the Gulf.[1]

These surging forces alternately and successively overrun the whole Missouri basin. Thus during one week Montana and the Dakotas may be covered by a blanket of moist air from the Atlantic and the Gulf while a few days later cold north air comes down and precipitates violent storms. Within a relatively short period dry southwestern winds may then parch the crops. Not only is the range of temperature extreme but both seasonally and secularly rainfall is variable. In spring the warm air from the Gulf will cause showers over thousands of square miles and occasionally a wedge of cold air meeting the warmer winds causes violent rain and hailstorms. As a result, a large percentage of the annual rainfall of any particular area may be deposited within a few hours, or a few days of spring rains may account for the bulk of the total precipitation for the year.

The implications of such variable weather over an area of half a million square miles are readily apparent from the point of view of floods and droughts. This is the basic reason why the Missouri Valley

[1]For readers who are interested in the subject of the weather, a fascinating study of climate and settlement in the Great Plains is included in the 1941 Yearbook of Agriculture, entitled *Climate and Man.*

and its auxiliary streams must be brought under control. The cycle of disastrous floods and droughts threatens the entire agricultural economy, and if uncontrolled might in time leave this area again a wasteland.

To bring the rivers under control and to eliminate the fluctuations in natural conditions which so disastrously affect the economy is in many respects the greatest problem facing the Middle West. To attack this problem and to provide the basis for a more stable and ultimately a more productive agriculture in the region, plans have been projected for harnessing the Missouri from its mouth above St. Louis to its remote source in southwestern Montana. In addition to those already built, scores of dams are contemplated. This construction would at once make possible the development of thousands of acres of new irrigation. It would improve inland navigation. On an even more elementary level it would guarantee adequate water for livestock as well as for human consumption in areas where thirst and grime are now normal through many days of the hot summers. Not the least of the projects which are proposed will be a system of canals. These would have the effect of raising the water level in the sandstone so that farmers instead of hauling water for miles, from water holes, would be able to have living wells of their own.

Considered in its entirety, the various Missouri Valley projects surpass the scale of the development in the Tennessee Valley. The drainage basin of the Missouri covers about 530,000 square miles or more than one-sixth of the total land area of the United States. The Missouri basin is thirteen times larger than the Tennessee basin and twice as large as the Columbia River basin. The water supply, however, is proportionately much less than in either of the latter regions. The annual yield of water of the Missouri system is slightly less than that of the Tennessee Valley system and far below that of the Columbia River. The conservation of the limited supply provided by the low rainfall over much of the area therefore becomes all the more important.

The benefits which might be anticipated from harnessing the Missouri include not only flood control, irrigation and new power but also soil conservation, the control of silting, the provision of more adequate municipal and farm water supplies and the development of navigation. The Bureau of Reclamation has estimated that a full development of the Missouri system as outlined in its plans recently submitted to Congress would furnish irrigation for 4,760,000 acres of new land and would provide supplemental water to nearly 550,000 additional acres. This area is equivalent to nearly 50,000 one hundred-acre irrigated farms which would represent a substantial increase in national wealth, considering the fertility of the land.

The Bureau of Reclamation points out that these figures represent a continuing benefit to the West far beyond the increment in crops in any particular year. The development would result in providing a stability in natural conditions which are now principal obstacles with which farmers in the region must contend. If the effects of erratic pulsation in the climate could be subdued by means of reservoirs and irrigation projects, the economic status and earning power of the farmers could be expected to show an immediate rise. It is not simply to rescue the acres which are now annually submerged by floods or burned by droughts, but to establish secure communities supported by regular and reliable agriculture that these programs are envisioned. In terms of dollars and cents, the Bureau of Reclamation believes that the tax base in the basin would increase in valuation by more than six hundred million dollars ($600,000,000) with development of these projects. Within the relatively short period of forty years the Government would receive some three hundred million dollars ($300,000,000) in repayment. Nevertheless, such returns are minor when compared with the significance of a stable and more prosperous population scattered in the valleys from Missouri to Montana.

The power developments of the proposed new dams run into very large figures. The Bureau of Reclamation believes that the firm annual production at proposed installations would amount to about 3,800,000,000 kilowatt hours. This output may be compared with about 9,500,000,000 kilowatt hours in the Tennessee Valley and about 9,000,000,000 kilowatt hours marketed by the Bonneville Power Administration from the various installations in the Columbia Valley. Although these power possibilities are less than half of that produced by other famous installations, yet they are almost as large as all of the electric energy now generated in the Missouri basin by coal, water power and gas. In 1941, for example, the power output in the Missouri basin was slightly above 4,000,000,000 kilowatt hours.

It is impossible to reduce to terms of dollars and cents some of the benefits which might reasonably be expected. It is certain that the prevention of floods alone, aside from the major purpose of a more stable economy, is a worthwhile objective. A Missouri flood commonly causes tens of millions of dollars of damage. Not only are crops lost for the year but fields are silted and graveled almost beyond redemption, especially in the lower reaches of the River. Moreover, there is no adequate dollar measure of the loss caused by floods in homesteads, livestock and possessions.

A summary in the report on the Missouri River basin by the Conservation Service presents some rather impressive estimates of the benefits which might be anticipated. The value of irrigation annually is estimated at one hundred thirty million dollars ($130,000,000). If the water resources of the Missouri basin are fully developed, the power generated would be worth seventeen million dollars ($17,000,000) annually, flood control another seventeen million dollars ($17,000,000), navigation and municipal water supplies together about five million dollars ($5,000,000), to make a total of nearly one hundred seventy million dollars ($170,000,000). The total estimated cost of these projects is about one billion two hundred sixty million dollars ($1,260,000,000), with a repayable balance of about seven hundred forty million dollars ($740,000,000). On purely economic grounds, therefore, these projects would appear to be good investments.[2]

[2]The benefits, costs and returns of the Bureau of Reclamation plans are set forth in Table XII, p. 163 of the Appendix.

Under the present plans the immense area of the Missouri basin is subdivided into several separate projects such as the Yellowstone, the Upper Missouri, the Fort Peck, the Platte River and the Lower

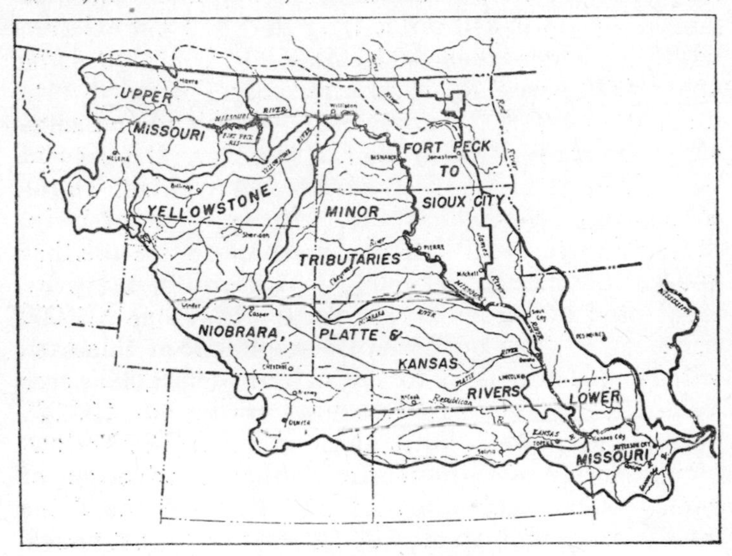

THE MISSOURI BASIN

Missouri. The plans for each area are fascinating for the promise they contain. The names of some of them have historic associations recalling the colorful stories of the early days in which the areas were first explored. In the Yellowstone area, for example, are the Big Horn Mountains, Wind River Basin, the Shoshone Reservoir, Pilot Butte, and the Yellowstone National Park. This is, of course, a region of geographic grandeur. Much of it rises more than 4,000 feet above the sea and plateaus at the 10,000 foot level are normal. Tablelands, buttes, escarpments are the familiar terms describing the landscape.

The Valley of the Yellowstone provides a good example of the scope on which development must be measured. It is 440 miles long and has a maximum width of more than 300 miles. It contains some 45,000,000 acres of economic value, divided into more than 40,000,000 acres of grazing land and some 4,000,000 acres of farm land of which, at the present time, more than a million acres are irrigated. In the Wind River Basin there are 210,000 acres of irrigable land. In the Big Horn area there are another 350,000 potentially irrigable acres, and in the principal part of the valley of the Yellowstone 310,000 acres more. The proposed development of this area will benefit new land to the extent of 509,000 acres and will provide supplemental water for 205,000 acres. The power plants at the dams in the Yellowstone Valley will have an annual production of nearly 600,000,000 kilowatt hours, while the dams in Wyoming will develop 900,000,000 kilowatt hours.

The Upper Missouri project tells the same story in terms of land development and the generation of electric power. The new land brought under irrigation will represent a total of nearly 670,000 acres. Power production at three dams would turn out 420,000,000 kilowatt hours annually. The watersheds of the Platte and Kansas Rivers in the four states of Colorado, Wyoming, Nebraska and Kansas contain a total of 1,300,000 acres which would be served, in addition to more than 2,000,000 acres already under irrigation.

If we look at the proposed power development of the Missouri Valley as a whole, twenty power plants are contemplated having an ultimate potential output of about 4,700,000,000 kilowatt hours per year. One of the principal advantages of the unified development of power over the Missouri Valley will be the network of power transmission lines which will link the several states. Connecting links will exist between the power plants northward from Nebraska through the Dakotas across Montana and diagonally down to Wyoming and Colorado. Thus, when one reservoir is low as the result of irrigation and drought, others are expected to be high because of the immense range of climate covered by the network and because of moisture variations in the mountains as compared with the plains. Consequently, the minimum or so-called firm power which will be available throughout the year is much greater in all localities than would be true if plants were isolated without interconnecting transmission lines.

Over much of the plains area the present cost of electric power is rather high. The range varies from 3.5¢ per kilowatt hours for residential power in Montana to 4.6¢ in South Dakota. For the region as a whole, the average price of residential power is 4.1¢ per kilowatt hour. This may be compared with a residential power cost in Washington, D. C., of about 2.4¢ per kilowatt hour. Power for industrial purposes in the Valley is also expensive, running higher than 1.62¢ per kilowatt hour for the whole area. This latter figure is nearly ten times the cost of commercial power sold by Bonneville, the average price of which is around 2 1/3 mills (the mill, of course, is equal to 1/10 of 1¢). Generally speaking, it is uneconomic to operate factories on 2¢

power, especially where they must compete with factories having a power cost of 2 or 3 mills. In making aluminum, for example, the power cost at Bonneville would be 2¢ a pound, while at an average rate of 2¢ per kilowatt hour in the Missouri Valley the power cost of aluminum would be 20¢ per pound, an obviously impossible figure. At present prices of electricity it must be taken for granted that few industries consuming much electric power will be built in the Valley.

Although estimates are not readily available for the cost of new power in the Valley, it is believed that the price will be sufficiently low to permit the utility systems of the cities to purchase power rather than to generate it by present methods. In many cases it is expected that rates would fall well below ½¢ per kilowatt hour. The cost of distribution which is substantial under average conditions in Western municipalities would, of course, be added.

A large percentage of the power produced in some localities will undoubtedly be used in pumping water for irrigation. Even after allowance for this purpose, however, there will still be an ample supply of power for cities, farms and new industries attracted to the area. When we consider that the power facilities of the Valley will be more than doubled by the proposed development, it is remarkable that the project was not undertaken long ago. The war awakened us to its necessity. It is our responsibility to see that so far as possible the plans are carried into effect.[3]

[3]The present and proposed power installations in the Missouri Basin are shown in Tables XIII and XIV, pp. 164, 165 of the Appendix.

From this standpoint it is indeed fortunate that the development of the Missouri Valley has in some degree passed the planning stage and is now supported, at least partially, by legislative authority. On February 28, 1944, the War Department, acting under authority granted by a resolution of the Committee on Flood Control of the House of Representatives, transmitted to the House a program prepared by the Corps of Engineers for the control of the Missouri River. This plan was directed primarily toward flood control and navigation improvement. According to some of its critics it did not give adequate consideration to the development of irrigation and hydroelectric power.

In April, 1944, the Bureau of Reclamation published its own plan under the title of "Conservation, Control and Use of Water Resources of the Missouri Basin." Many of the facts and figures which have been used in this chapter have been taken from this report. Because of conflicts in the reports of the two agencies a joint committee was appointed to reconcile differences of fact as well as of opinion. This reconciliation was embodied in a report to Congress in November, 1944, so that it may be now safely said that so far as the record goes, the War Department and the Department of Interior are in basic agreement on the broad plans.

The reconciled plan prepared by the two agencies was approved by Congress in Section 9 of the Flood Control Act of December 2, 1944. The Corps of Engineers was authorized to expend up to two hundred million dollars ($200,000,000) toward the construction of the initial phases of the flood control and navigation programs. The Bureau of Reclamation was authorized to spend another two hundred million dollars ($200,000,000) in the development of the initial stages of irrigation power and related programs for the Valley. Although these expenditures will extend over a period of years, in sum they represent a long stride toward the ultimate goal.

In February, 1945, Senator Murray introduced a bill to set up the "Missouri Valley Authority" intended to unify the development of the Valley under the program somewhat similar to that of TVA with such modifications as required by the different problems involved. This bill has been under consideration by three committees of the Senate: the Committee on Commerce, Committee on Irrigation and Reclamation, and the Committee on Agriculture and Forestry. Whatever the fate of particular legislation may be, the questions posed by the Missouri Valley cannot be avoided in the long run.

It should be made entirely clear that the present discussion of the development of the Missouri Basin attempts no evaluation of the detailed plans and makes no suggestions concerning the administration of whatever authority Congress may grant. What should be borne in mind is that some steps are already under way and that in all likelihood much more will be done in bringing the rivers under control and in smoothing out the great fluctuations in the seasonal flow of the streams.

To the Mountain States and to the Plains States any program with these objectives is vital. Such a program, in its principles, is of equal concern to the nation as a whole. The physical and financial returns of economic development are material and readily reckoned. We can see and count homes, cars, factories, and farms. Yet there are qualities and rewards that accompany such transformations of environment which cannot be easily enumerated, or even easily defined. Rising incomes will bring more education. More education nearly always results in greater productivity, and with it the pursuit of achievement in spheres which may be closed or unrecognized when labor is expended unprofitably, or capital lacks the stimulus to enterprise, or land steadily deteriorates. It is the lesson of all the lost land in this country that the erosion of the soil is recorded in diminishing returns to diminished hopes.

How different it is when an area has been attuned to the lives of the people who dwell there. By accommodating nature and aiding its adjustments the land is given a new economic balance, often superior to that which existed before men disturbed the soil or by their shortsightedness invited the havoc of floods and the wasting of fertile earth. When people have acknowledged their debt to nature by flood control, and have harnessed the strength of the rivers for electricity instead of permitting periodic displays of unguided force, an almost magic change occurs. Land, industries, and people develop in ways that would not have been possible before. Activity and accomplishment are heightened and acquire an outward proportion which is the visible sign of an economy that is both free and in equilibrium.

That all these results are attainable we know from the splendid performance of TVA, and from the stimulus to industry and agriculture given by Boulder, Bonneville, and the Grand Coulee. It bears repeated emphasis that such efforts open new vistas for private enterprise. In a free enterprise system it is a proper function of the people, of government, and of industry to cooperate in providing the basis upon which enterprise can gain a solid footing, and competition can operate in new directions. This is not economic planning in the ordinary sense. Rather, it is a reasonable attempt to make enterprise effective by removing conditions which prevent initiative from being exercised. Only then can the play of competition become as fully creative, profitable, and efficient in the multiplication of goods and services for wide markets, as it can be when it is released from unnecessary handicap. From that point forward, the vigor and resourcefulness of the people will do the rest.

CHAPTER X

The Railroads

TRANSPORTATION is the lifeline of the American economy. The history of this country can be told in the story of the means by which the continent has been economically united by waterways, turnpikes and rails. As the covered wagon and the pony express gave way to the railroads, and as the development of canals and turnpikes speeded inland communication, the trade and commerce of the country grew. All of us are familiar with the turbulence and scandal of the early railroad era but we also know that this era produced the thousands of miles of track which created a national economy and made possible the rise of our industrial civilization.

Space and distance have dominated the lives of people in the West. Hence transportation is a vital and recurring theme in Western history. Because the conditions of transportation will influence the success or failure of all of the programs intended to stimulate Western industry, it is necessary to obtain as clear an understanding as possible of the factors and problems which affect the transportation pattern. In transport as in so many other spheres of Western development the old has mingled with the new, both in technical advancement and economic policy. Alongside the railways, the pipelines, the water carriers and the trucking which served the Western part of the United States before the war, there are now two other types of service which have grown rapidly in the last few years and will enormously enhance the transportation facilities available to Western industry in the future. These new additions are Western shipping and air transport. It is perhaps not too much to say that air transport can have the same significance for the West in years to come that railroads had several generations ago. Fundamentally, however, the transportation problem in the West is the problem of the railroads. For the foreseeable future, rail transport will largely determine the conditions under which Western industry as a whole is to operate.

In such a tangled skein of economic affairs as transportation the simplest, most forthright facts may be deceptive in appearance. On the surface it would seem that in a domain equipped with thousands of miles of railroads, truck highways and pipelines, great ports, inland navigation and increasing air facilities, competition both among the forms of transport and individual operators would be continuous and intensive. If this were so, we could reasonably expect measurable results. There would be a studied, incessant drive for increased efficiency. There would be a perceptible lowering of rates under pressure of the market. Constant effort would be made by all varieties of service to attract and hold patronage with the maximum quality and quantity of operation which the market could sustain. The value of the service and the principle of what the traffic will bear would produce an ever widening and deepening market. Such competitive effects would be marked in those branches of transport in which alternative methods were available as, for instance, where the shipper has a choice between air and rail. Within each field, moreover, the public would at all times know that every carrier was prompted by competition to provide the best possible service at the lowest possible rates.

These agreeable conclusions will not withstand the test of fact. The moment that inquiry proceeds beyond the physical level it clearly appears that there is superimposed upon the potentially competitive basis of the transport system a hierarchy of rate structures, monopolistic practices, and outmoded policies which represent the accumulated restraints of decades. Until the war the inertia which characterizes a monopoly-ridden industry permeated transportation. Technological progress and genuine competition between newer and older forms of transport were held in check and, in some instances, almost nullified. Increase in the range of transport service for the most part brought no real abatement in rate discriminations. The war strained the machinery of these arrangements to the breaking point. Their inadequacy became obvious. It became even more evident that such a monopolistic pattern is an impossible foundation for a strong, well-articulated and efficient regional economy, now or in the future.

Both as a production center and as a market the West has had to contend in the past with a freight rate differential, with monopolistic practices and with regional discriminations which have retarded its economic development. Nor is it the West alone which has felt the effects of such restrictions. Transportation is so interwoven with the processes of production and distribution that every article of commerce, and the pocketbook of every consumer, is touched at some point by transportation cost. As products move through the channels of trade to the ultimate consumer, the transportation factor which enters into the early states of extraction or fabrication is often multiplied and pyramided many times. A charge of one dollar ($1.00) for freight on the movement of a unit of raw material may impose an additional cost of two ($2.00) or three dollars ($3.00) on the ultimate consumer.

As an economic principle it is as true today as it was in the days of Adam Smith that transportation fixes the limits of the market, both physically and financially. The distance between the farmer, the manufacturer, the merchant and the consumer is measured not only in miles but also in rates. Differentials which may appear small by themselves often prove to be the decisive element in the production of a commodity or in the ability of the consumer to purchase it. Moreover, an imbalance in transportation cost among the various regions of the country will over a period of time affect the equilibrium of the entire economy.

If excessive freight rates depress the productive ability and purchasing power of one area, the results are felt by manufacturers and consumers in other areas. It is today no more possible to isolate the final impact of discrimination than it is to localize a depression. It has been futile in the past and it will be futile in the future to build plants or to seek capital in the West, no matter how rich the natural resources, if the handicap of transportation cannot be overcome. At the same time, in dwelling at some length on the problem of rail transport, it should be emphasized that from the standpoint of the ultimate welfare of the carriers themselves, as well as the regions which they serve, the unremedied persistence of discriminations which have grown up over the years will lead to conditions requiring much more drastic action than the removal of artificial differences indicated at the present time.

The rail carriers are truly the arteries of American commerce. If the areas which they serve are economically sick, they cannot function over any long period of time without also becoming affected. On the other hand, if by changes in present practices the railroads make possible a burgeoning of Western industry, they will increase the source from which they draw their own sustenance and will profit thereby.

From the standpoint of rail transport the United States is divided, like ancient Gaul, into three parts. These three major rate regions are known as the Eastern Territory, the Southern Territory, and the Western Territory. The latter territory comprises roughly the area west of the Mississippi River and includes approximately 72% of the geographic area of the country. Of the total 233,277 miles of track operated by class 1 steam railways in the United States (as of December 31, 1939) nearly 131,347 miles or 56% lie within the Western Territory.

The Western rail carriers are generally divided

into four major groups: the Southwestern-Gulf route, the Granger route, the Transcontinental route, and the Pacific Coast route. The Southwestern-Gulf route links St. Louis and Kansas City with Gulf points in Texas and Louisiana. Within this area there are both transcontinental and intra-regional rail lines, such as the Missouri Pacific; the St. Louis and Southwestern; St. Louis and San Francisco; the Southern Pacific; the Missouri, Kansas and Texas; the Chicago, Rock Island and Pacific; the Kansas City Southern; and the Atchison, Topeka and Santa Fe. The bulk of traffic by rail in the northern area of this region flows through Kansas City and St. Louis. In general, this traffic radiates from a number of cities, such as New Orleans, Memphis, and Cairo, and Beaumont, Houston and Galveston in Texas. Carriers in this area are supplemented by other agencies of transport such as water, highways, and pipelines.

The Granger route lies north of the Southwestern-Gulf route and like the latter is served by both transcontinental and intra-regional railroads. Here, also, rail carriers are supplemented by highways and pipelines, although water transport is relatively unimportant. In general, rail competition in this area is potentially keen because of the "checker-boarding" effect produced by north-south carriers cutting across the lines from east to west. The carriers serving the Granger region radiate principally from St. Louis, Chicago, Milwaukee, and Duluth. The principal rail centers in this region are Minneapolis and St. Paul, Omaha, Kansas City, Sioux City and Des Moines on the east, and Pueblo, Denver, Cheyenne and Great Falls on the west.

The transcontinental route extends westward from the Southwestern-Gulf and Granger routes to the Pacific Coast. This route has three principal divisions. The northern branch includes the Northern Pacific, the Great Northern, and the Chicago, Milwaukee, St. Paul and Pacific lines. The central Transcontinental route comprises the Union Pacific and a combination of the Missouri Pacific and the Burlington with the Denver and Rio Grande and the Western Pacific. The south Transcontinental route is made up of the Atchison, Topeka and Santa Fe, and lines of the Southern Pacific, the St. Louis Southwestern and the Chicago, Rock Island and Pacific. All of these routes must compete with water transport through the Panama Canal. The three routes are rather widely separated but they converge at a number of centers such as Portland and the Puget Sound cities on the Pacific Coast and at Minneapolis, St. Paul and Chicago in the east. During the war these three transcontinental routes were called upon to transport a tremendous volume of westbound war material from the industrial areas of the East and Midwest to the Pacific Coast for reshipment to Pacific combat areas.

The Pacific Coast route, as its name indicates, is principally concerned with traffic between California ports and the cities of the Northwest, such as Portland. The Pacific Coast route is served chiefly by the Southern Pacific, the Western Pacific, and the Santa Fe as far north as San Francisco and Sacramento.

A comparative picture of the volume of traffic in 1939 (which is used as the last so-called normal year before the war) indicates that in the area covered by the Granger, the Transcontinental, and the Pacific Coast routes, the railroads supplied 52% of the total tonnages. Of the remainder, highway transport accounted for 18%, waterways 21% and pipelines 9%. In terms of revenue ton-miles the railroads hold 70%, water carriers 18%, highway carriers 8%, and pipelines 4%.

This sketch of the rail network of the West has been drawn in some detail, for it is against this broad canvas that a discussion of freight rates acquires meaning. It is essential in examining freight differentials to distinguish between class rates and commodity rates. Class rates apply to groups of goods which are generally related, of comparatively limited bulk, of comparatively high value. Commodity rates apply to heavier goods carried in large quantities, such as coal, livestock, or cement. There are three major railroad classifications and five major rate territories applicable to rail traffic. These classifications and rate territories developed on a regional basis, and may be explained in part by the fact that comparatively few railroads within one classification region cross the boundaries of the other regions.

In somewhat simpler terms this means that in the East, involving the area bordered by the Mississippi River on the west and the Ohio and the Potomac on the South, the Eastern or Official Classification governs the class rate scale. This scale is then applicable to traffic moving within the Eastern zone. In the South, which embraces the territory east of the Mississippi River and below Official Territory, the Southern Classification applies. The rest of the country is governed by the Western Classification, which includes three principal class-rate territories: the Western Trunk Line, the Southwestern, and the Mountain Pacific. Within each of the major rate regions there are several subdivisions or "subrate" territories.

All freight class rates are based upon percentages of a stipulated first-class rate which represents 100%. Every article tendered for shipment is then assigned a rating within a particular classification. In other words, a percentage of the first-class rate is applied on all articles listed, in all of the three classification territories. The class rate tariffs, however, name the actual rates on the commodities within the classification. To illustrate, let us assume that the first-class rate between two points within Western Territory is one dollar ($1.00) per hundred pounds while the particular article offered for shipment between these two points is rated at Class 70. The class rate on the article offered for shipment would accordingly be 70¢ per hundred pounds. Thus the classification gives the rating while the freight class tariff gives the specific rate.

Commodity rates, on the other hand, are published to apply to specific articles. In general, commodity rates are lower than concurrent class rates but they are predicated upon so many different bases and levels that it is virtually impossible to draw any broad conclusion as to their average percentages of first-class rates. It is usually recognized, however, that most of the tonnage transported in carload quantities by rails moves on commodity rates. This is especially true with respect to low grade commodities such as sand, gravel, logs, coal and ore. According to a study made by the Interstate Com-

Major freight rate territories and relative levels of intraterritorial class rate structure

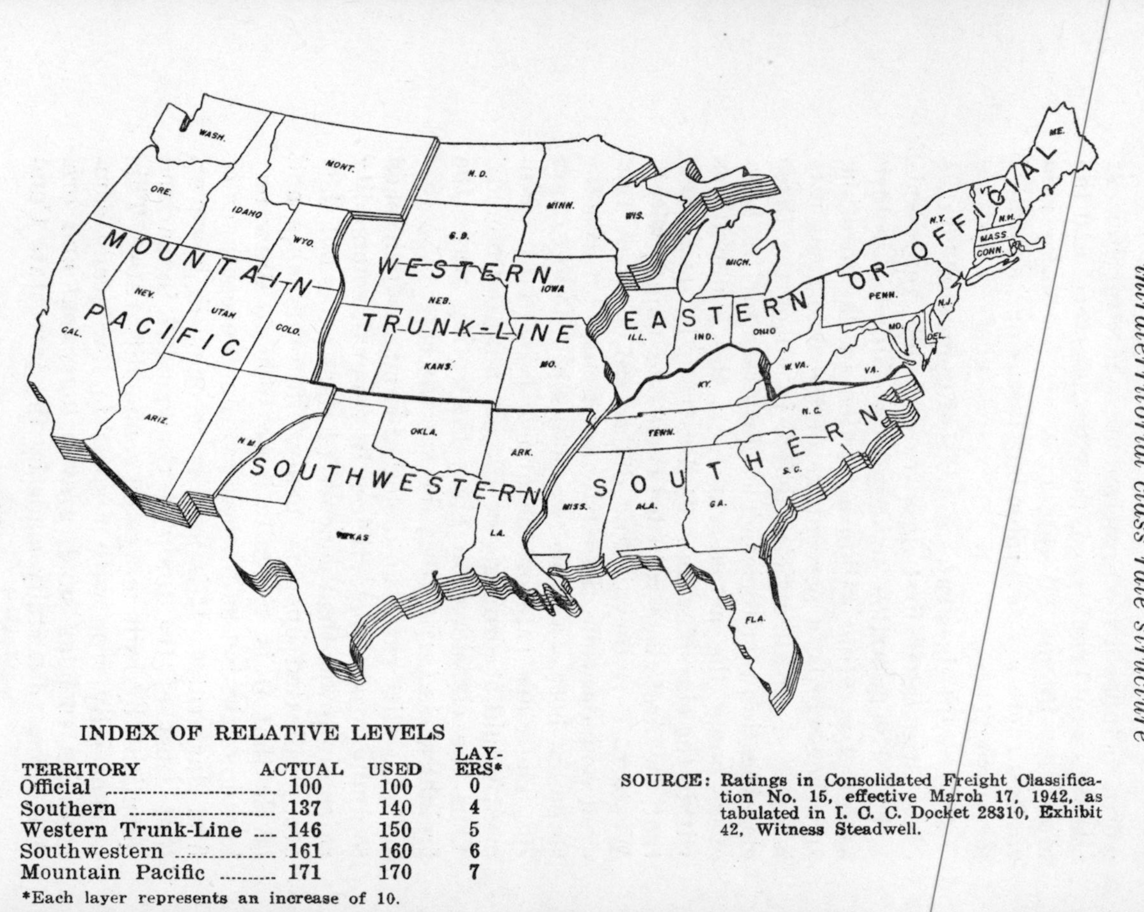

INDEX OF RELATIVE LEVELS

TERRITORY	ACTUAL	USED	LAYERS*
Official	100	100	0
Southern	137	140	4
Western Trunk-Line	146	150	5
Southwestern	161	160	6
Mountain Pacific	171	170	7

*Each layer represents an increase of 10.

SOURCE: Ratings in Consolidated Freight Classification No. 15, effective March 17, 1942, as tabulated in I. C. C. Docket 28310, Exhibit 42, Witness Steadwell.

merce Commission it was found that only 4.1% of all carload traffic originating on all the railroads for a one-day period in 1943 moved on class rates under normal classification ratings, while 10.7% of all carload traffic in this same period moved on classification exceptions. By far the greater part of carload traffic, or 85.2%, moved on commodity rates.

The traffic moving from a point in one classification territory to a point in another, thus involving an interterritorial movement, generally comes under a single classification. It should be noted, however, that the three major classifications are not uniform with respect to the ratings on listed commodities. Indeed, these differences in ratings are frequently very substantial. They constitute one of the principal reasons for which the present regionalized rate structure has been subject to attack by Western and Southern interests, because their classification ratings on innumerable commodities are higher than comparable ratings in Eastern Territory.

The rate structures in the South and West have also been on a higher level than the East. For example, if the Official or Eastern Territory is taken as 100 the levels in other territories are generally as follows: South 139, Western Trunk Line 128 to 184, Southwestern 161, and Mountain Pacific 166. In attempting to market finished goods in the East that move on class rates the shippers of the South and West are at a substantial disadvantage, mile for mile, in comparison with the rates available to producers shipping in the Eastern or Official Territory.

On the average, goods subject to class rates, which are primarily important in the marketing of industrial products, must pay rates 37% higher in the South than for comparable service in the East. In the West these rates are from 46% to 71% higher than in the East. The importance of class rates lies in the fact that they apply particularly to manufactured goods, so that the effect of a differential must inevitably be reflected in the distribution of manufacturing industries.

Consequently, on both a class and a commodity basis the agriculture and industry of the West have worked at a definite disadvantage. In this sense it is not extreme to speak of "the colonial system," for the net effect of differentials is to place a burden upon finished articles manufactured in the West when they are shipped to other territories, and to favor the import of finished articles from the East. A few instances will make clear the paralyzing effects of such discriminations. For example, the rate on work clothing in carload lots from Macon, Georgia, to Chicago, a distance of 817 miles, is $15.60 per thousand pounds as compared with a rate of only $11.20 from Philadelphia to Chicago, a haul of 814 miles. From Omaha, Nebraska, to Columbus, Ohio, a distance of 748 miles, the comparable rate is $18.70 per thousand pounds while the rate is $15.20 from Fitchburg, Massachusetts, to Columbus, a distance of 743 miles. From Denver, Colorado, to Evansville, Indiana, a distance of 1,083 miles, the freight rate is $29.40 per thousand pounds as compared with a rate of $18.40 from New London, Connecticut, to Evansville, a distance of 1,088 miles. Examples of such disparities among the principal rate territories could be multiplied almost endlessly.

The West and the South have long fought against these high and discriminatory freight rates. Until very recently the battle has been waged without victory or effect. To both regions continuous disadvantage in transport cost has meant not only the loss of local industry and the inability of new industry to rise. It has meant a perpetual reduction in purchasing power, a gradual drift of population to more favored regions and, in some sections, it has meant even the closing of schools and the loss of homes and farms. Bitter experience has taught the people of these regions a basic lesson—that it will avail them little to build factories, to develop power projects, to seek new industries and new capital unless the slow poison of transport handicaps can be eliminated.

CHAPTER XI

How Rates Are Made

THE CAUSES of discrimination are many and varied. Some of the factors present fall into the category of historical accidents, that is, differences which were attributable to the original economic conditions among different regions of the country. The original differences may have long since disappeared but the early distinctions have continued to affect rate making, and to influence the location and character of industry. In other cases there are clearly defined efforts on the part of special interests to obtain initial preference. In some cases, such as that of the rebate system, the successful efforts by monopoly groups to acquire and maintain privileged positions, even though later nullified by law, have nevertheless left a lasting imprint on the transportation fabric. It must be kept in mind, therefore, that in seeking out the causes of rate discrimination the object of inquiry is not obloquy or accusation. Rather, it is an analysis of the laxity, both public and private, which has tolerated for so long fundamental inequities in transportation costs.

It has long been a widespread belief on the part of the public that all rates and charges of railroads and other common carriers are fixed by the Interstate Commerce Commission. This body was created in 1887 to regulate various aspects of transportation, primarily as a safeguard against the continuation of abuses on the part of the railroads in the period following the Civil War. Subsequent legislation has gradually extended the responsibilities and powers of the Commission. There is no question that throughout its career the Interstate Commerce Commission has succeeded, in the main, in the purposes which it is intended to serve. In many respects, indeed, the Interstate Commerce Commission is often considered the outstanding example of what a regulatory agency should be, and its rulings, tested in practice over the years, have by and large had a salutary effect upon the development of the American transportation industry.

With respect to rates, however, the function of the Interstate Commerce Commission has generally been misunderstood by the public. The Interstate Commerce Act, as it now stands, makes it the duty of every common carrier to initiate its own rates and to file them with the Commission. The Commission in reviewing the rates thus made by the industry cannot and does not ordinarily go behind the given data to consider whether the rates are arrived at by agreement or compulsion or, in relatively rare instances, open competition. Investigations conducted by the Department of Justice indicate that more than 99% of the rail rates filed with the Commission become the "lawful rates" without any review by the Commission. In the 1% of rates that are reviewed by the Commission the questions at issue relate primarily to whether the rate is within the zone of reasonableness under the Interstate Commerce Act and whether the rate violates any other specific provisions of that Act. The Commission has the power to conduct general nationwide or territorial investigations and to establish rates in accordance therewith, but such investigations are quite aside from the daily routine of rate making and from the processes by which rates are initiated.

How, then, may we account for the persistence of excessive and discriminatory rates and rate bases? Why has not the natural force of competition over a long period of time operated to equalize or at least to minimize rate differences? The principal clue which leads us to answers to these questions is found in the existence of some sixty private rate associations and rate conferences throughout the United States which constitute the rate making machinery of the railroad industry. Before any rate is filed with the Interstate Commerce Commission and thereby becomes the "lawful rate", it must first find its way through the intricate series of committees maintained by the rate associations and conferences. In effect, this private rate making machinery is so geared that it has been able to exercise virtually complete control over the pricing of transportation services. This pyramid of private rate making agencies is headed by the Association of American Railroads which may be considered more or less the parent body of regional rate making groups, having jurisdiction over the East, the South and the West.

It is especially interesting, therefore, to devote

some attention to the manner in which private rate making has affected the economic fortunes of the West and to present briefly the means which were employed by a private group to determine Western railroad rates. In 1932 a scheme called the Western Commissioner Plan was superimposed upon the already elaborate rate bureau or price fixing mechanism among Western railroads. This plan, known as the Western Agreement, was signed by thirty-five railroads operating west of the Mississippi River. Within the compass of the agreement were included a number of organizations having special spheres of influence and exercising different degrees of control. Under the agreement all of them became subject, in varying extent, to the general control of the Western Traffic Executive Committee.

This agreement created the Office of the Western Commissioner, who was responsible to no public authority. He was charged with the duty, among others, of arbitrating proposed changes in rates and practices which might adversely affect the earnings of the signatory railroads as a whole. In general, the Western Commissioner exercised appellate jurisdiction with respect to the rulings of the Western Traffic Executive Committee. If his decisions were not accepted, the Commissioner reported that fact to a Committee of Directors. While the agreement is silent on the duties of this committee, there would seem to be little doubt concerning its role. The members of the committee represent the "financial interests" in the railroad industry and its meetings were convened in the auspicious climate of 40 Wall Street. At these meetings the Western Commissioner reported, "as to any questions adversely affecting net revenues arising among any of the railroads in the Western District upon which it has not been possible to secure unanimity of action by the interested railroads." It is indeed a rather remarkable picture of the formulation of transportation policies that is presented by this system.

The basic attitude of the Committee of Directors under the Western Agreement toward rates was stated succinctly in a resolution passed by them in 1938: "Resolved: that without passing on the merits of the particular case under consideration the Directors' Committee expressed the view that, in the interests of the Western railroads as a whole, there should be no bidding for traffic on a rate basis." A few examples will illustrate some of the ways in which this attitude was manifested. In 1933 the Missouri Pacific lines, in connection with the Denver and Rio Grande Western, decided to lower freight rates in order to meet existing truck competition by establishing so-called "all-commodity" freight rates between St. Louis and Kansas City and Denver. On January 26, 1933, the Interstate Commerce Commission granted permission to publish the rates on ten days' notice. The Union Pacific, the Rock Island, the Burlington, and the Santa Fe protested against the cheaper rates. The Western Commissioner of railroads was able to report on January 2, 1934, that

> "after giving this subject careful consideration, conclusion was reached that it would be adverse to the interests of carriers as a whole in Western Territory, and that the rate proposed should not be established. This conclusion was accepted by the proponent line, the Missouri Pacific Railroad Company."

As might be expected, the lower rates were not put into effect.

In 1933 the Chicago Great Western decided that it would reduce rates on various packing house supplies and products between Chicago and Missouri River points. The Western Association of Railway Executives passed a resolution on October 2, 1933, declaring that the proposed reduction by Great Western

> "is unwise and would be disastrous to the net revenues of all the roads serving the territory affected by the proposed reduced rates in that it would adversely affect all other rates and result in the loss of revenues to the interested roads as a whole, in excess of any possible recovery of traffic taken from the railroads by motor truck competition; and that the Committee considers that such action cannot, consistent with the interests of the industry as a whole, be taken by one railroad independently and contrary to the judgment of the Commissioner and all other interested railroads."

After a series of conferences the Chicago Great Western withdrew its proposed reduction.

Similar instances of the direction in which decisions on rates made under this system appear ordinarily to have tended are found throughout the history of the Western Commissioner Plan. It would seem logical to conclude that such instances represent something of a settled policy. It requires no irony of understatement to interpret the remarks made by the Western Commissioner upon another occasion. In 1933 an unusually heavy peach crop in Western Colorado, Utah, and southern Idaho combined with distressed market conditions produced strong appeals to the railroads to reduce rates in order that the fruit might move to market. These appeals were met by divided opinion on the part of the railroads. Some of the lines were willing to reduce rates but others protested. The Western Commissioner decided that the rates should not be reduced. He stated

> "I pointed out that railroad rates cannot be adjusted to keep pace with the various fluctuations in crop, industrial and economic conditions and the principle that overproduction on a given commodity is not a justifiable reason for requiring rail carriers to reduce reasonable rates. I therefore recommend that the proposal be not placed in effect on the ground that there is no justification for the proposed reductions and their inauguration would result in the dissipation of the railroad revenues and consequent prejudice to the public interest."

The consistency of policies and views set forth by the Western Commissioner is further amplified in an excerpt taken from the Commissioner's summary of his activities in the year 1934. In this review it is stated:

> "In order to meet a situation in the Pacific Northwest territory resulting from the increased use of other types of fuel, the Union Pacific Railroad announced its intention of reducing rates on fuel from southern Wyoming and Utah points into that territory, which it is alleged would have the effect of stimulating coal traffic. This action was protested by other Pacific Northwest lines on the ground that such reduction would fail to accomplish the purpose desired and would result in a loss of revenue to all participating carriers. Following the conference at which all phases of this matter were considered, report and conclusion was rendered, recommending the withdrawal of the tariff reducing the coal rates by the Union Pacific."

The scope of the Western Agreement was, of

course, not restricted to rates. In the course of its operation problems involving technical improvement of carriers, new types of service and competitive schedules were also encountered. They were decided in accordance with the general objectives and spirit of the agreement. In consequence improvements in railroad equipment were delayed, new services were curtailed and proposals to speed up freight and passenger schedules were regarded askance. Thus, for instance, after the Western Agreement became effective the Chicago, Burlington and Quincy Railroad wrote to the Western Commissioner concerning the installation of air-conditioning equipment in dining and club cars. It was apparently contemplated that air conditioning should be limited to such equipment in order to avoid a repetition of what happened between Chicago and St. Louis, where all passenger cars on four trains in each direction had been air conditioned. With respect to this matter the Western Commissioner wrote to the Southern Pacific on January 9, 1933, that

> "Air conditioning appears to be an innovation which the public is demanding and I presume the Western roads will desire to keep abreast of other territories in its adoption. However it seems very probable that if something like a uniform policy could be determined upon, a very considerable sum of money might be saved."

In response to this suggestion an executive of the Southern Pacific replied,

> "It is unquestionably desirable that the Western lines should air condition their trains to the same extent as their connections in the East have done but in view of the uncertainty of light passenger traffic dur-

ing the coming summer . . . it would seem to be best to postpone for another year any extension of air conditioning except as some lines may find it necessary to air condition more of their dining cars."

Such activities are important only because they indicate a point of view fundamentally hostile to progress and specifically inimical to competitive development in transportation service. It may seem a relatively minor incident, for example, that the Western Commissioner was active in persuading the Burlington to slow down a new freight schedule which it had placed in effect between Denver and Fort Worth. It may seem trivial that the Commissioner was able to persuade the Missouri Pacific to abandon a proposed freight schedule which would have brought perishable goods from California to New York twenty-four hours earlier than the customary schedule, or that he was able to keep the Chicago and Northwestern from eliminating a charge for furnishing heater service on shipments of potatoes. It is, however, in their sum and in their cumulative effects that such practices, whether deliberately conceived and executed or accepted and followed as a matter of custom, have subordinated the economic position of the West to the maintenance of a system of discrimination. Moreover, as a result of these practices and other similar restraints on competition in the railroad field in general and the West in particular, the position of the railroads themselves will inevitably be jeopardized in the long run. Their equipment both in quality and quantity would become deficient. The lack of change and progress in efficiency and price of their services will certainly in the long run weaken them in any effort to keep pace with the pressure of newer forms of transportation.

The Western Agreement of course is only a small part of the attempt by railroad carriers in the United States to eliminate competition. Mention should be made of the Transcontinental Freight Bureau which is a powerful agency within a powerful agency—the Western Traffic Executive Committee. The Transcontinental Freight Bureau makes transcontinental rates for the entire nation. There are twenty-three member railroads of which nine, a minority of the members, exert effective voice in rate making. This Bureau has original jurisdiction over rates on transcontinental freight even though it moves to, from or through the territory of one of the many other private rate agencies. No purpose would be served by dissecting in detail the complex anatomy of this or similar organisms which have grown up in the railroad industry. It is enough to recognize that the system as it actually works is a system of private rate making; that private rate making is conducive to discrimination and that discrimination is the key to the transportation problem of the West.

Shortly after the Department of Justice uncovered the existence of the Western Agreement, a copy of it was requested. This occurred on April 9, 1943. On April 14, 1943, a copy was received by the Department and one was also filed with the Interstate Commerce Commission—about eleven years after its original execution. Nine days later, on April 23, 1943, the agreement was purportedly canceled.

Following investigation of the arrangements which have been discovered to exist, the Department of Justice filed a complaint in the United States District Court at Lincoln, Nebraska, charging violations of the Sherman Act by the Association of American Railroads, officers and members of its Board of Directors; the Western Association of Railway Executives; J. P. Morgan and Company; Kuhn, Loeb and Company; forty-seven railroads and their chief executives and thirty-one other individuals. The Attorney General stated at the time

> "The complaint filed today charges that a combination of private financial, industrial and railroad interests have acted collusively to maintain non-competitive rates for transportation and to prevent and retard improvements in the services and facilities of railroads for the western part of the United States. It also charges that the defendants have retarded and suppressed the development and growth of the motor carriers and other forms of transportation competitive with the railroads in the Western area."

In addition, the defendants were charged specifically, among other things, with conspiring to impose upon shippers in the Western District freight rates higher than those fixed in the Eastern District; with hindering technological progress; and withholding from the public the benefits of expedited freight and passenger service.[1]

Regardless of the outcome of this particular case or similar cases arising under the antitrust laws, it would seem clear in principle from an economic standpoint that restrictions and discriminations maintained by private agreement are the least desirable of all possible methods of resolving the

[1]*United States v. The Association of American Railroads, et al.*, Civil No. 246, United States District Court, District of Nebraska, Lincoln Division.

transportation problem. Rate policies may determine the location of industry, the sources from which raw materials can be drawn, the markets to which finished products may move, the possibilities of geographic shifts of population and industry, and the opportunities for both improvement and enterprise within all regions. Even though prosecution under the antitrust laws may do much to remove private restrictions in the transportation field, there is a matter of basic economic policy which the American public and its Government must decide. A free competitive economy cannot operate if the chief arteries of trade and commerce are subject to the decision of private monopoly groups or if interregional discrimination places handicaps in the way of parallel development by the various sections of the country. What has been said here applies principally to the West and to the South, but it is nevertheless true that even though the East may seem temporarily favored by freight differentials, the long-run interests of all three areas coincide. All three have an important stake in transportation.

CHAPTER XII

Transport and New Industries

EVEN THOUGH all of the threads of cause and effect which enter into the transport problem were to be unraveled far more completely than they have been in this brief survey, predictions of the future would still necessarily be matters of conjecture. There are too many intangible elements involved to lend certainty to discussion. Nevertheless, an appraisal may be made of the effects of transport on new industries in the West, as well as a few estimates of changes which have some coefficient of probability.

While it is not possible to foretell accurately the terms on which the passage of goods to and from the West is likely to occur within any given period, there are a few signs which suggest the course of public policy. One of the principal indications of the direction in which public policy is tending is contained in the report of the Interstate Commerce Commission issued on May 15, 1945. This agency conducted an investigation of rail and rail-water class rates in the portion of the United States east of the Rocky Mountains and rail and rail-water freight classification for the entire country. Commodity rates were not included in the scope of the study.

In its findings the Commission set forth the principles to be considered in making interim adjustments in rates and the objectives to be sought in permanent adjustments. The rulings dealing with interim adjustments contemplate:

1. A reduction of 10% in the class rates applicable within Southern, Southwestern and Western Trunk Line territories, between these territories, and between Official Territory and the specified territories.

2. An increase of 10% in the existing class rates applicable within Official Territory.

3. The interim class rates to be governed by existing classifications.

For the permanent adjustment there are provided:

1. A uniform freight classification for the entire United States based on the Official Classification with additional classes added.

2. A uniform scale of class rates for the part of the country located east of the Rocky Mountains, which is to approximate 115% of the basic class rate scale in effect in Eastern Territory.

The interim adjustment is to remain in force until a uniform classification is prepared, preferably by the rail lines with the assistance of the shipping public and state regulatory bodies. The railroads have indicated their willingness to prepare a uniform classification. Presumably when the carriers have completed the compilation of a uniform classification, both the uniform class rates prescribed by the Commission and the uniform classification will become simultaneously effective.

It should be noted that these rulings apply to class rates so that the amount of traffic covered by the Commission's decision is relatively small. It is important to the South and the West, however, because so many manufactured goods move under class rates. Such traffic in the South and West will accordingly under the permanent adjustment be carried on at the same level as traffic within the Official Territory. In effect, this adjustment will represent the realization of a goal for which shippers in the South and West have been struggling for many years. Moreover, uniform class rates will provide the groundwork for uniformity or perhaps, more aptly, equity in other types of rates. Such further relief would seem to be implicit in this step.

There remains, however, a tremendous distance to be covered if the root causes of differentials are to be removed. Not only public policy but the voluntary action of the railroads, the conditions of the market in general and the bargaining relationship between shippers and carriers must be propitious if existing disadvantages are to be overcome. This is especially true with respect to the emergence of new industry and to the continuation of Western plants which contributed so greatly to war production.

During the war period transportation costs to shippers in Western Territory were secondary to the necessities imposed by a national emergency. The question of rate disadvantages was consequently subordinated. Now that newer economic interests and new enterprises must make their way under peacetime conditions the rate handicap becomes decisive.

A recent instance offers clear illustration of the type of difficulty which may be expected. The case in question involved a number of Midwestern meat packers, including some of the Nebraska packing plants, that were financed with public and private funds to assure adequate output of food in the war effort. In its decision the Interstate Commerce Commission stated that the rates at issue did not permit the free movement of meats from the Midwest to the Pacific Coast. The Commission asserted that there was no logical reason for the greatly different relation between Westbound and Eastbound rates and prescribed substantial reduction in the rates on fresh meats and packing house products from Omaha, Nebraska to Portland, Oregon, Seattle, Washington and San Francisco. As the Commission stated,

> "The Omaha packer could not reach New York with his meats at rates 249% of those on the live animals, nor can he do so on that basis to Los Angeles . . . The rate on packing house products from Omaha to Los Angeles is 191.7% of the rate on the live animal, but to New York it is only 99.7% of that rate."

Such a problem is, however, relatively simple when compared with the questions affecting the production of such commodities as steel, tin plate, fabricated non-ferrous products (such as copper, lead, and zinc items or ferro-alloys) and aluminum, magnesium or chemical commodities. Plants built during the war may not in all cases have been located in the most ideal sites from the standpoint of their continued operation. Their operating costs, the terms on which they may be disposed by Government to private operators and basic price conditions affecting their market possibilities were not in all cases adequately calculated in terms of peacetime production. Assuming that these difficulties are surmounted, however, transportation rates are still the dividing line between their success or their failure.

Thus, for instance, although it is inevitable that the steel plant at Geneva, Utah, must reckon with the apportionment of potential Western markets with Eastern producers, a revision of rates is critical if the plant is to enjoy reasonable participation in Western trade and at the same time be free from monopolistic control. The plant at Geneva offers the greatest possibilities for the production of tin plate, terne plate, tubes and other steel products to meet the substantial and increasing demand in the West. Twenty per cent of all the tin plate used in the United States is consumed in the West and there is, therefore, a solid basis upon demand to be anticipated. Despite this a recent survey by the Attorney General reported to Congress on June 24, 1945, indicated that the rate factor may well be crucial. The report stated with respect to the Geneva plant that

> "Disposal to Eastern steel interests, especially those with water access to Western ports would substantially lessen competition and could retard the development of Western facilities. It cannot be too strongly emphasized that successful operation depends upon railway rates which will reflect the competitive advantages of location and bear logical relationship to transportation costs on raw materials (ore) and semi-finished materials (pig iron) moving within or into the region. The own-

ing agency (Defense Plant Corporation) should use every effort to establish a reasonable commercial rate prior to disposal. This is especially imperative to the prospects of interesting independent purchasers."[1]

In this connection it cannot be ignored that previously existing rates and rate relationships on steel products are prohibitive for competition by Geneva with other production areas of the country. Iron and steel articles, including tin plate, fall into the fifth class in the Official Classification. It is notable that the rates in the Western region in 1939 were higher than in any other section of the country. This was indicated by a study made by the late Board of Investigation and Research in Transportation. It was found, for example, that for 500 miles the applied rates between points in Official Territory averaged 34.7¢ per hundred pounds as compared with 51.4¢ between points in Western Trunk Line Territory and 48.1¢ between points in Mountain-Pacific Territory.

Similar disparities will influence the extended operations of Western producers and fabricators of copper, lead and zinc products and other potential peacetime producers. Some types of production are of course more favorably situated than others. The aluminum and magnesium interests, for instance, have available tidewater facilities along the Pacific Coast and may well be able to establish favorable bargaining positions with rail carriers to effect rate adjustments. It is possible also that relocation and decentralization will substantially improve the position of many new industries both in respect of their costs of production and their market relationship

[1]Senate Document 95, 79th Cong., 1st Sess., p. 27.

to the railroads. Increasingly also as public policy develops to maintain competition among the various forms of transportation, the pressure upon the railroads from truck transportation, water lines and air shipping will grow greater.

It is obvious that no complete solution to the transport problem of the West is immediately available. It is equally obvious, however, that unless Western industry, with the help of Government, public opinion and the railroads themselves, is able to work out an acceptable and effective program, the full economic development of the West will be indefinitely postponed. It is the responsibility of Western interests to make certain that this does not happen. It is a prime requisite for the well-being of the national economy that the transportation requirements of the West as well as those of the rest of the country be aligned with the necessities of the future.

CHAPTER XIII

The Sherman Act and the West

DURING the years of the war the American economy has operated on the principle of necessity. The primary aim of victory has determined economic policies. In all its phases economic activity has been carried on according to a system of priority. Every step of production, distribution and consumption has consequently been subject to some degree of wartime regulation in the form of price controls, rationing and other measures which were absolutely required to make possible the survival of a democratic way of life.

With the achievement of victory these wartime regulations have largely been relaxed. In fact they have been lifted at a rate much more rapid than at first seemed possible, with the exception of those modified safeguards necessary to prevent a runaway inflation or to bridge the gap between war needs and the resumption of peacetime production.

Quite understandably it would come as a great shock to the American people if they were told that the entire system of restrictions, directives and priorities by which Government guided the war economy were to be continued into the indefinite future. No administration would propose to maintain in peacetime any such complete Governmental direction of economic life. It would not take very long for the American people to vote out of office any party which sought to regulate the entire economy in the years of peace.

If monopoly has its way, however, we shall enter the period of peace with a business structure highly organized and directed from the top—a structure in which orders are given by a relative few who control economic policy. Those who benefit from and consequently advocate the organization of industry on monopoly lines would like to determine what and how much shall be produced. They would like to decide whether a product shall be made at all, and if so, who will be permitted to make it. They would like to choose how products are to be transported and on what terms, and ultimately they would like to decide who shall be allowed to buy and sell and at what price.

The great difference between the blueprints projected by monopoly and the Governmental regulations required by war is that the program of the monopolists acknowledges no public responsibility, stems from no public authority, and provides no protection for the public interest. It is, in other words, a system of private economic government. The monopolist wants an ordered and secure market. He wants to be protected against the competition of new processes and new enterprises. He wants to regulate production and distribution, not in accordance with the priorities of war, but rather on the basis of privilege and preference. To the monopolist the power to control necessarily means the exercise of discrimination.

Even though this picture is drawn in black and white it is not an exaggeration. We may feel that the American public would not long tolerate an economic system in which private monopoly groups exercised such final authority over the country's economic life. It must be realized, however, that monopoly has, in all too many instances, acquired proportions which approach this condition. It is for this reason that the threat of private monopoly is today the major obstacle to the successful functioning of a free economy.

It is at this point that the antitrust laws assume critical significance for the maintenance of a system of free enterprise. It is important, therefore, that all American citizens, perhaps especially the people of the West, should understand exactly what the Sherman Act is, what it is supposed to do and how it is applied.

The Sherman Antitrust Act was passed over half a century ago, in 1890. Its essential provision states that "every contract, combination in the form of trust or otherwise, or conspiracy, in restraint of trade or commerce among the several States or with foreign nations is hereby declared to be illegal." In its origin the Sherman Act was a product of its times. It set forth in unequivocal terms the reaction of Government and the general public against the domination of economic life by the old trusts. In a more profound sense, however, the Sherman Act affirmed the principles of common law and economic custom upon which our society is based. It elevated to the level of national policy the historic conception that restraints of trade, whether they are imposed by monopoly or by the various devices of combination, violate the freedom of opportunity.

To the West the antitrust laws represent one of the principal instruments not only for eliminating subjection to monopoly power but also for attaining greater economic independence in the years ahead. In the future, even more than in the past, the West must be concerned that the program of monopoly shall not prevail. If it does so, the West will be in many ways a greater loser than any other area. The seats of monopoly power are not in the West. The industry of the West is not an interest that entrenched monopoly groups wish to preserve. Quite the reverse. To a considerable extent it is the potential competition of Western industry that monopolistic groups in our economy would like to control or to eliminate.

Necessarily the impetus and drive for the creation of new local industries must come from the people of the West themselves. Their efforts would be stultified, however, even under the most favorable conditions, if their new industries were vulnerable to covert or open attack by monopoly. The enforcement of the antitrust laws is vital if there are to be strong, new and independent enterprises in this region.

One of the most impressive features of antitrust enforcement is that results are measurable, not only in the removal of collusion or the freeing of price structures, but also by the emergence of new business concerns. To the West this can mean the rise of independent packing houses scattered throughout the livestock area; the formation of local companies to process fruits and vegetables; the appearance of new concerns that are not mere branch houses to be closed at the will of absentee owners. From both a positive and a negative standpoint Western industry and Western consumers have much to gain through vigorous antitrust enforcement. As producers they will be freed from the stifling effects of monopoly upon economic development. They will be at liberty to strive for the development of new markets and to reduce prices to stimulate demand for their products. As consumers they will benefit by increased purchasing power and more opportunities for employment.

There have not been a great number of cases arising under the Sherman Act which originated in the West. There have been, however, numerous cases involving the national market in which Western interests have been both directly and indirectly affected. Thus, for example, a case involving a trucking association on the East Coast may concern the fruitgrowers and shippers of the West, by raising prices of fresh fruits and vegetables to consumers in the Eastern area to a point where the market is restricted, with a consequent decrease in the return received by Western farmers. A case involving the manufacture of flat glass, which includes plate glass, safety glass and window glass, has immediate relevance for the West even though all of the producers concerned are located in the East. The West Coast is one of the principal markets for flat glass products. Because of the elimination of competition in the flat glass industry and the division of the national market among a few major producers the

West does not have any glass factories of its own. At the same time because of the price fixing and marketing arrangements existing in the industry Western consumers have been compelled to pay monopoly prices for the glass products which they used.

One or two special instances may be described to illustrate how the antitrust laws work and why the West has at all times to be alert to the growth of monopoly conditions. The first case demonstrates how collusion affecting the national market necessarily affects Western industry. The second case will serve as an example of the way in which international cartel arrangements have frequently controlled the production and distribution of Western commodities.

A few years ago the Department of Justice initiated action against the National Retail Lumber Dealers' Association and twenty-two state and regional associations of retail lumber dealers. These associations included in their membership about twenty thousand lumber dealers throughout the United States. Because of the prominence of the lumber industry in the West many Western firms were members of the various associations and consequently figured as defendants in the case.

The complaint charged the various defendant associations with violations of the antitrust laws through a program of restricted distribution in the sale of lumber, lumber products, cement and other building materials. According to the complaint such materials were sold only through "recognized" retail lumber dealers who were members of the associations and who adhered to the market practices which the associations sought to enforce. The defendants in this case were charged with conspiring to suppress competition, to fix prices, to allocate territories and customers and with seeking to compel manufacturers and wholesalers to refuse to sell to dealers who were not included in the arbitrary roster of "recognized" firms.

The decree resulting from antitrust action enjoined the defendants from engaging in any further plan to allocate markets or customers, or to fix prices. The defendants were also prohibited from attempting to exert pressure against manufacturers and wholesalers for the purpose of discriminating against particular producers or customers. A large number of those named in the complaints were also required to pay fines. The effects of such action are of course economic as well as legal, so that not only are defendants placed under obligation to abandon monopolistic practices but the market itself is relieved from the burden of artificial restraints. Economically it may be said that the principal effects of this case were to render retail lumber prices much more fluid than they had been, and at the same time to free independent dealers from the discrimination to which they were previously exposed.

The effects of cartel agreements on the West have been much more important than is generally realized. If a statute were passed which provided that with the exception of a few specified firms no company on the West Coast would be permitted to export to Latin America or to the Far East and no shipping line would be permitted to carry products of Western companies to these markets, the impact upon Western industry would be regarded as catastrophic. Yet this is precisely what private cartel agreements have done, even in industries in which the West is most favorably situated.

The antitrust action involving the borax industry gives a clear-cut picture of the degree to which cartel control can be fastened upon an important branch of production. In 1944 seven corporations engaged in the business of mining, processing, manufacturing, selling and distributing borates, borax and boric acid, were indicted for violation of the Sherman Act. The defendant firms were specifically charged on the following grounds:

1. They acquired control of virtually the entire world supply of crude borates, borax, and boric acid by acquisition and by trade practices which drove out or prevented competition by American concerns.

2. They allocated foreign and domestic markets and customers.

3. They agreed upon restrictive selling and distributing methods and fixed prices at which products were to be sold.

In some respects this cartel was unique, because practically the entire world supply of borax and boric acid is produced from raw materials mined in the State of California. Borax products have a wide range of commercial outlets and technical uses. They are employed as fluxing agents in refining metals, in the manufacture of antiseptics, enamels, glass, starches, aviation panels, explosives, steel, rubber, fuels, leather goods and pharmaceutical products.

The raw materials, the manufacture of finished products, the trade within the United States and foreign commerce were all subject to the monopolistic and price fixing agreements of the cartel. It was especially significant, moreover, that one of the principal defendants in this case was found to be substantially owned by German interests. Investigation of this cartel led to the seizure of the German-owned stock by the Alien Property Custodian. There were, of course, a number of defendants, some of which were American firms while others were controlled by interests outside the United States.

The control of cartels over world business and the control of the national market by domestic monopolies are equally inimical to Western industrial progress. The enforcement of the antitrust laws against the American participants in cartel agreements can do much to nullify the effectiveness of cartels. Our courts have jurisdiction over the acts of American cartel members and they also have jurisdiction over the acts of foreign members when they take place in this country or when they directly or indirectly restrain American commerce. Our experience indicates conclusively that cartels could not perpetuate their control over world industry without the cooperation of American companies, and it is the settled policy of this country, as it is embodied in the Sherman Act, to combat the participation of American firms in such combines.

It has been even more apparent that our smaller businessmen have nothing to gain and everything to lose by aligning themselves either with gigantic foreign interests bent on complete industrial control or with schemes designed to eliminate competition in the domestic market. When the problem of monopoly and all that it implies for our economic and political life is properly debated and understood by businessmen, there is not the slightest doubt of their desire to resist any attempt to fasten a monopolistic system upon our economy. On the contrary, there is every indication that when businessmen, as well as the public at large, become aware of the inroads which monopoly and cartel control have made on competition they are united in their demand that the Government proceed actively to restore a free market. The importance of this objective to small business and to local and regional business will increase rather than decrease in the period immediately ahead, for we are now aware that monopoly grows most rapidly in the unsettled market conditions which follow a war.

The pattern of industrial organization which will exist in this country in the coming years will of course depend a great deal upon Governmental policies. It has already become evident that in the process of reconversion the Government will pursue every effort to reverse the wartime trend toward concentration and to foster the conditions which make competition in industry a reality. Even though legislative and administrative policies in the disposition of Government-owned plants and of surplus materials and capacity are designed to promote independent enterprise, the role of business itself is crucial. In fact, it may be said that so far as the West is concerned the realization of its inherent capacities, even with the aid that Government can offer, ultimately rests upon the decisions which Western capital and Western industry adopt and support with all the resolution at their command. If this is done, there can be little doubt that the economy of the West will achieve every promise which its resources and its energies hold forth.

CHAPTER XIV

New Horizons

A GREAT CIVILIZATION is manifestly possible to America and the world in the decades that lie ahead. Despite the wars and depressions of this century, which have so shaken the foundations of national life and international understanding, it is now in the power of mankind to create a world in which many of the root causes of such historic tragedies are removed. The meaning of victory is the opportunity to work toward this end.

The culmination of World War II has found this country in the process of rediscovering the values and purposes which motivated its establishment: to be a free nation within a free world. In this respect there is today a renewed awareness of the essential principles and the major aims, both political and economic, which form the framework of our national life. At the same time, it has become increasingly clear that we still have far to go, not only in the realization of our purposes but in forming the instruments by which they may be achieved in an era of industrial marvels and economic complexities. No more important fact can be kept in mind in the vexing interim of reconversion than that the economic stature of this country is not fixed. The way in which American industry and labor met the grim challenge of war demands gave us new insight into the possibilities of our economic development. It became apparent that there were many areas of enterprise still to be explored, many resources to be tapped and many more skills and talents available for the task than had been realized.

With the attainment of victory, the success of the American economy in coping with the problems of a new era may well be decisive. The political structure of peace must rest upon a secure economic basis. One of the principal contributions which this country can make, both to itself and to the rest of the world, is the development of genuine prosperity.

History has thrust us to the point where we must seize upon the strategic facts of our economic life and free that life from the clustering usages which limit, rather than nourish and support its growth. The economic philosophy to which this country is committed by its traditions as well as by its desires is a philosophy of freedom and action. The principles of political liberty to which we adhere are paralleled by the belief that the prime mover of economic activity is freedom of the market. The assumptions which underlie our national economic policies are derived from an instinctive feeling that freedom is politically and economically interdependent. It is this conception which defines the ends we seek to serve in combating the growth of monopoly power in our economy.

It is to be hoped that the evidence presented throughout these pages makes clear that the continuing crux of both the industrial policies of Government and the behavior of industry itself pivots upon the presence or absence of monopoly. The triumph of monopoly would in time become the nemesis of our system of free enterprise. Domination of the market, regimentation by private economic governments, and all of the attendant varieties of discrimination which characterize monopoly are not only paradoxes to be examined academically; they are a menace whose perpetuation we cannot brook.

The events of recent years have increasingly underscored the fact that there is a direct and profound association between the existence and power of monopoly in our economic system and the failure of Western industry to evolve and to expand as it could and should. The effects of monopoly on the West have in some cases been remote and subtle, and in others immediate and obvious, but they have been everywhere persistent and insidious when judged by the degree to which Western industry has been discouraged or stifled. Almost continuously since the period of its early exploration the West has been subjected in one way or another to all the artifices of monopoly and to all of its effects.

Both as a producing and a consuming area, the West has felt the consequences of monopoly domination of important industries. The raw materials of the West have been shipped to the East for fabrication and then shipped back to Western markets. As a result a vicious circle has operated to limit opportunities for the improvement of industry and labor in the Western States, at the same time that Western consumers have been compelled to pay higher prices for the commodities which they required.

Western enterprise and Western capital could not enter such fields as chemicals, aluminum, magnesium, steel or electrical equipment on competitive terms. These industries, like so many others, were governed by national monopolies or subject to the ministrations of international cartels. In numerous instances in the years before the war the efforts of Western businessmen to enter attractive sectors of production encountered an impenetrable wall of monopoly or cartel control.

On frequent occasions it was the decision of cartel groups to prevent the establishment of industries in the West. The power which such groups wielded rendered their verdicts notoriously effective. No matter how much vision or initiative or technological skill or capital were marshaled for the purpose, Western industry found that it could not engage in production unless monopoly was willing. With respect to competition monopoly is habitually unwilling, and independent action in many cases was practically impossible. In effect, this meant that only in special circumstances and at rare intervals could new concerns in the West arise in an industry ruled by cartels. If a new concern were established, its survival was predicated upon the whim of monopoly and contingent upon the calculated restrictions by which cartels attempted to preserve their privileges. It is indeed remarkable, when we consider the degree to which monopoly prevailed before the war over whole spheres of technology and over world markets, that Western industry was able to progress as far as it did.

To a considerable degree the enforcement of the antitrust laws in recent years and the stringencies imposed by war have loosened the grip of monopoly from many of the most important sectors of industry. Unavoidably, the concentration of economic power has in some ways been accelerated by the pressure of war needs and in the course of expediting war production. This concentration, however, has taken place under the open scrutiny of Government and the Public. It is reversible by the exercise of forethought in the process of reconversion. Thus if a reasonable proportion of the war plants and industries which have been built in the West can be continued in operation on terms of independence from monopolistic control and equality in transportation costs, there is every ground for belief that the West can compete on merit in these branches of production. It is even more apparent that the removal of cartelism in industry will make possible and feasible the emergence of new types of enterprise in the West, based upon both older raw materials and more recently developed resources and techniques.

It would be a fundamental error for the West to consider its problems in any solitary abstraction from those of the national economy. It would be an equally grave mistake for the nation at large to hope for the attainment of prosperity unless the problems of the West are solved. At the present time the struggle of the West is primarily a struggle against monopoly and against all the modes and forms of economic discrimination. But such a conflict is neither novel nor unique; it is a concern shared by other regions, both in the past and at the present time.

If we look back at history in the light of current urgencies, it is apparent that in its economic aspects the American Revolution was a revolt against monopoly. Throughout the Nineteenth Century the separate states fought to keep the market free. From one standpoint the settlement of the West itself often obscured the effects of monopoly and diverted attention from the need to combat it. As long as opportunity could be found in the opening up of new areas, the dangers inherent in trusts and combines were not so evident as they were later to become. It was not until the passing of the geographical frontier, when the continued concentration of economic power threatened to eclipse enterprise, that Government was aroused to the recognition of monopoly as a formidable opponent.

The opposition of the people as expressed in the development of the Populist and Granger movements in the post-Civil War era finally led to the passage of the Sherman Act. Even though account was taken of the long-run implications of monopoly for the American economy, by the enactment of a law designed to eliminate restraints of trade, the enforcement of the law was more nominal than real. Indeed, in the halcyon days of the Twenties, when size became the symbol of efficiency in industry, and industrial mergers became not only the fashion but a frequently eulogized trend, the purposes of the Sherman Act and the validity of its formulation were almost forgotten. This occurred, moreover, in the same period in which the cartelization of world industry reached a peak.

Ineluctably, the tolerance of monopoly and cartel domination of economic life contributed first to a fantastic boom and then to its inexorable sequel, the Great Depression. Even then, however, relief was sought not so much through efforts to free the market as to shift the locus and the purposes of control. The N. R. A. was born of good intentions, but its economic premises were faulty because they sanctioned, in effect, the cartelization of industry which had fostered the collapse.

Only at a relatively late hour in our history, during the latter part of the Thirties, did we become fully aware of the meaning of monopoly and fully awakened to the need for vigorous enforcement of the antitrust laws. This effort was admittedly tardy. Yet, it was surprisingly effective. Among the first and greatest rewards of enforcement were the exposure and the elimination of the hold which international cartels had gained upon many of our strategic industries. As a result of the findings made during the years of the war, there has been swift recognition on the part of the public, as well as on the part of industry and Government, that the enforcement of the antitrust law ranks today among the foremost concerns of this country. We have already seen something of their significance to the West.

As we contemplate the difficulties and the possibilities which lie in the future, it may seem that the perplexities which overshadow current events and blur the lines of policy cannot be dispelled in sufficient time to forestall the recurrence of depression or the scaling down of industrial activity in the West to a pre-war level. It may be said also that these perplexities have been described only in miniature in this review. Nevertheless, it has been and remains a basic conviction that, given a chance, the West will be able to develop as its capacities indicate that it should.

The possibilities which have been sketched cannot come into being overnight nor without resolute cooperation. There are many things that Government can do in assisting and promoting the industrial development of the West. There are many things that business, and labor, and capital can and must do if the advances which have already been made are to be carried over into the years of peace. This is true not only in the relationship between the West and the American economy as a whole, it is true also in the relationship between Western industry and world markets. The West is on the border of the great Pacific basin. The successful revival of world trade through international cooperation will open ten thousand miles of markets in the Orient to Western producers. The countries of Asia which have been stricken by war and which are seeking, like the West, to develop their own resources will need innumerable commodities and will prove to be eager purchasers of every type of product which the West can make.

Again, the shape of world trade and therefore the promotion of Western trade with the Orient, with South America, with Canada, with Australia, and with other world markets will be very much dependent upon the curbing of cartels. The phenomenal growth of Western shipping and the advent of air transport as a large-scale international carrier place the West in an exceptionally favored position to reach world markets. Ability to do so will mean nothing if cartels and trade restrictions close Western industries at the source, or shut them out of markets without a chance to compete. Before the war, not only Western producers, but whole American industries were often prohibited by cartel agreements from trading in South America, China, and other areas. But if, through the Good Neighbor Policy, the Reciprocal Trade Program, the enforcement of the antitrust laws, and policies of economic cooperation with the United Nations, cartels are deprived of their dominance and trade restraints are reduced to a minimum, we can expect the expansion of world trade to a volume greater than the past has ever known. To the West, such a development would be among the most powerful incentives for industrial development that could be devised. Pending any final solution of the trade problem on the world-wide level, however, we can at least do our best to carry out the policies of competition and free enterprise in our own economy, and in our own international dealings.

There is as much assurance as there can be of anything in an imperfect world that the economic growth of the West will be steadfast if our perspectives are well-drawn. With the other regions of the country the West shares a common destiny. The economic future of the West cannot be separated from the economic future of the South or of the East, for they are all equally committed to the success of a national venture in achievement. Both on its own behalf and as part of American society, the aim of the West should ever be to promote and defend an economy in which the gates of opportunity are open to new business enterprises, new products and processes, and to new men with new skills. As producers, as entrepreneurs, as workers, and as consumers Westerners will gain opportunity as the American economy becomes more free, more active, and more progressive, or lose it if the American economy becomes concentrated, static, and averse to progress. There can be little question as to which alternative the West wants, or which way the East and the South desire to go. The important point is that unless they march together, it will be difficult, if not impossible, for this country to attain prosperity. For American capitalism to function successfully in a period of world upheaval, and for the American people to know that they will have opportunity to build for themselves and their children a more abundant society, the principles of economic freedom must be practised.

This means that trade among the States and sections must move without barriers of transport or discrimination. It means that capital in Maine, or California, or Nebraska, must have equal opportunity for investment in new industry. It means that a monopoly which seeks to suppress new enterprise or invention, whether in Oregon or Kansas, is also striking a blow at the economic welfare of Tennessee and Pennsylvania.

The West is once more the frontier on which the question of America's economic expansion will be decided. All its trails have not been blazed. Even though its mountains have been mapped, its rivers charted and its elements classified, the full economic greatness of the West is undiscovered. It need not remain so. If the West recognizes its own right to grow and acts upon that recognition, and if the rest of the country understands how deeply the common interest will be affected by what happens in the West, discovery will soon follow.

As they look toward tomorrow, the people of the West have a heritage of natural resources to work with, the will of the pioneer to get things done, material reward to work for, and a vision of the future to infuse their striving with a sense of dignity and meaning. In return for assistance and encouragement extended to it by other sections the development of the West will constitute a magnificent addition to the industrial strength and economic welfare of America. This is as it should be, for the West is, after all, a part of "this region, this soil, this clime" which compose the United States.

APPENDIX

Table I

Summary of Cost of Production at Aluminum Plants Owned by the Defense Plant Corporation, 1944

(Cents per Pound)

Mill	Total Operating Costs[1]	PRINCIPAL ITEMS OF COST: Alumina	Power	Labor	Carbons	Production (Millions of Pounds)
Jones Mill (Ark.)	11.9	4.7	4.0	1.0	1.0	134.1
Troutdale (Ore.)	11.3	5.7	2.0	1.4	1.2	104.8
Spokane (Wash.)	11.0	5.5	1.9	1.1	1.2	191.7
Tacoma (Wash.)	15.8	5.7	2.0	2.6	0.9	36.7
Los Angeles (Cal.)[2]	13.2	5.6	3.8	1.5	1.1	72.7
Riverbank (Cal.)[2]	15.0	5.6	4.4	1.5	1.3	43.9
Massena (N. Y.)[3]	15.4	5.6	7.3	1.1	1.1	9.1
Maspeth, Long Island (N. Y.)[4]	15.4	5.6	5.7	1.3	1.4	86.5
Burlington (N. J.)[2]	15.8	5.4	5.8	2.0	1.2	22.4

[1] Before depreciation, general overhead and taxes.
[2] Production suspended in August (average for 8 months).
[3] Operations as a DPC facility suspended after January 1944. Cost figures are for month of January only.
[4] Production suspended in May (average for 5 months).

Table II

Value of Important Agricultural Products of the Western States and Percentage Relation to the United States Total, 1942

(In Thousands of Dollars)

	Cattle and Calves	Sheep and Lambs	Wool, Shorn	Wheat (Farm Value)	Sugar Beets
Western States					
Arizona	$ 27,844	$ 2,008	$ 1,602	$ 667	....
California	89,365	21,378	9,821	11,304	$17,257
Colorado	66,848	26,387	5,809	28,962	14,157
Idaho	19,959	16,096	6,745	21,393	7,424
Kansas	169,325	14,584	2,250	225,385	....
Montana	43,251	19,535	13,186	75,996	6,359
Nebraska	134,740	14,846	1,512	78,996	5,450
Nevada	10,038	2,751	2,142	518	....
New Mexico	38,594	6,282	5,854	4,957	....
North Dakota	37,835	6,900	3,411	160,333	....
Oregon	25,683	7,925	5,040	21,350	....
South Dakota	54,159	10,816	6,405	48,443	....
Utah	14,102	11,086	7,941	5,110	3,890
Washington	21,043	4,266	2,088	56,802	....
Wyoming	21,056	16,259	12,995	4,417	2,794
Total 15 Western States	773,842	181,119	86,801	744,633	57,331
Total U. S.	2,305,019	308,062	157,235	1,077,762	79,538
Percentage 15 States to Total U. S.	33.6%	58.8%	55.2%	69.1%	72.1%

Source: U.S.D.A. Agricultural Statistics, 1943.

Table III

STAND OF SAW TIMBER IN 1938, PRODUCTION OF LUMBER IN 1940 AND ESTIMATED VALUES (BASED ON 1940 MILL VALUES)

(Quantity in Millions of Board Feet)

	1938 Total Stand of Saw Timber	1940 Lumber Production (Softwood)	Average Mill Price	1940 Value of Production	Estimated Value of 1938 Total Stand at 1940 Value
Total U. S.	1,763,651	24,903[1]	$22.48	$559,819,000	$41,128,341,000
Western softwoods					
Total	1,216,182	14,027	22.56	316,416,900	33,395,851,980
Douglas fir	489,905	7,121	19.49	138,788,290	9,548,248,450
Ponderosa pine	224,904	3,613	24.29	87,759,770	5,462,918,160
True fir	121,737	121	18.05	2,184,050	2,197,352,850
Western hemlock	115,551	716	22.19	15,888,040	2,564,076,690
Spruce	62,821	402	26.84	10,789,680	4,370,115,640
Redwood	39,150	389	40.35	15,696,150	5,614,702,500
Lodgepole pine	38,620	47	19.01	893,470	734,166,200
Western larch	25,306	131	16.03	2,099,930	405,655,180
Sugar pine	24,684	363	30.28	10,991,640	747,431,520
Western white pine	18,333	1,124	27.87	31,325,880	510,940,710
Others	55,171	....	22.48	....	1,240,244,080
Western hardwoods	4,957				

[1] Softwood only.

Table IV

ESTIMATED CHANGE IN CIVILIAN POPULATION IN THE WESTERN STATES DURING THE WAR

State	Estimated Civilian Population Apr. 1, 1940	Estimated Civilian Population Nov. 1, 1943	Change April 1, 1940 to November 1, 1943 Number	Change Percent
West of the Rockies				
Arizona	497,068	569,357	+72,289	+14.5
California	6,868,065	7,881,694	+1,013,629	+14.8
Idaho	524,809	473,166	—51,643	—9.8
Nevada	108,761	130,637	+21,876	+20.1
Oregon	1,088,284	1,172,674	+84,390	+7.8
Utah	549,722	583,572	+33,850	+6.2
Washington	1,719,143	1,905,239	+186,096	+10.8
Total 7 States	11,355,852	12,716,339	+1,360,487	+12.0

Table IV (Continued)

	Estimated Civilian Population Apr. 1, 1940	Nov. 1, 1943	Change April 1, 1940 to November 1, 1943 Number	Percent
East of the Rockies				
Colorado	1,119,274	1,067,095	—52,179	—4.7
Kansas	1,794,950	1,678,722	—116,228	—6.5
Montana	558,270	470,033	—88,237	—15.8
Nebraska	1,313,438	1,176,023	—137,415	—10.5
New Mexico	530,662	490,119	—40,543	—7.6
North Dakota	641,692	536,510	—105,182	—16.4
South Dakota	642,682	544,866	—97,816	—15.2
Wyoming	244,745	235,739	—9,006	—3.7
Total 8 States	6,845,713	6,199,107	—646,606	—9.4
Total 15 States	18,201,565	18,915,446	+713,881	+3.9
Total U. S. (Civilian)	131,329,104	127,307,884	—4,021,220	—3.1

Source: U. S. Department of Commerce Special Report on Population, February 15, 1944.

Table V

Percentage Control of Mine Production of Copper in the United States

Companies	Percent of Total 1920	1930	1940	Jan. 1943
Kennecott	4.13	12.96	40.45	43.2
Anaconda	16.34	18.78	20.48	18.9
Phelps-Dodge	5.57	7.95	17.88	22.4
Total 3 companies	26.04	39.69	78.81	84.5
All other	73.96	61.31	21.19	15.5
Total U. S.	100.00	100.00	100.00	100.00
Total U. S. mine production (short tons)	635,248	710,690	878,086	1,090,818[1]

[1] Total for year 1943.

TABLE VI

VALUE OF IMPORTANT MINERAL PRODUCTS IN THE WEST COMPARED WITH TOTAL UNITED STATES, 1943

State	Copper	Gold	Silver	Lead	Zinc
Arizona	$104,827,060	$ 6,013,350	$ 4,063,210	$ 2,059,050	$ 4,250,232
California	2,278,120	5,191,480	433,120	873,000	400,896
Colorado	267,280	4,814,530	1,894,501	2,704,800	9,524,304
Idaho	604,240	1,078,280	8,320,128	14,468,550	18,728,712
Kansas	....	....	....	1,381,950	12,299,904
Montana	34,976,500	2,085,510	6,009,152	2,448,600	8,122,896
Nebraska	....	....	....	....	....
Nevada	18,477,680	5,055,470	1,152,199	718,500	2,947,752
New Mexico	19,802,380	194,705	329,659	858,450	12,857,184
North Dakota	....	....	....	....	....
Oregon	1,560	38,395	7,483	600	....
South Dakota	....	3,725,540	25,519	6,150	9,936
Utah	84,237,140	13,666,450	6,740,864	9,788,550	10,129,536
Washington	1,901,900	2,283,540	263,424	753,300	2,635,848
Wyoming	....	....	....	....	....
Total 15 States	$267,373,860	$44,147,250	$29,239,259	$36,061,500	$ 81,907,200
Total U. S.	[3]282,434,000	48,808,270	[4]29,482,793	[3]61,537,000	[3]135,511,000
Percentage 15 Western States to Total U. S.	94.7%	90.5%	99.2%	58.6%	60.4%

Table VI (Continued)

Value of Important Mineral Products in the West Compared With Total United States, 1943

	Mercury (Metal)	Petroleum	Natural Gas	Clay Products	Potassium Salts (Potash)
Arizona	$ 105,609	....	....	[1]$ 200,000	....
California	6,600,440	$ 301,300,000	$119,250,000	14,000,000	[2]............
Colorado	....	2,600,000	1,385,000	700,000	....
Idaho	831,790	....	....	[1]100,000	....
Kansas	....	127,400,000	46,550,000	[1]700,000	....
Montana	....	9,500,000	8,480,000	[1]150,000	....
Nebraska	....	600,000	....	[1]400,000	....
Nevada	893,476	....	....	[2]............	....
New Mexico	....	38,400,000	14,450,000	[1]120,000	$21,918,503
North Dakota	....	....	58,000	[2]............	....
Oregon	907,922	....	....	500,000	....
South Dakota	....	....	2,000	[2]............	....
Utah	....	....	966,000	[1]1,000,000	[2]............
Washington	....	....	....	[1]900,000	....
Wyoming	....	32,400,000	6,993,000	[2]............	....
Total 15 States	$ 9,339,237	$ 512,200,000	$198,134,000	$ 8,770,000	$21,918.503
Total U. S.	10,137,060	1,812,560,000	753,810,000	75,200,000	26,183,073
Percentage 15 Western States to Total U. S.	92.1%	28.3%	26.3%	11.7%	83.7%

[1] Estimate.
[2] Not shown separately.
[3] Includes war bonuses.
[4] Total production of 41,460,826 fine ounces at $0.7111 per ounce.
Source: Minerals Yearbook, 1943.

Table VII

Resources of Bituminous and Subbituminous Coal in the Public-Land States as Compared with the Total United States

(Tons)

	Bituminous	Subbituminous	Total
Colorado	212,617,000,000	104,000,000,000	316,617,000,000
Idaho	[1]244,000,000		244,000,000
Montana	2,609,000,000	62,850,000,000	65,459,000,000
New Mexico	18,810,000,000	1,863,000,000	20,673,000,000
Utah	87,976,000,000	5,152,000,000	93,128,000,000
Wyoming	30,310,000,000	590,000,000,000	620,310,000,000
Total, 6 public-land States	352,566,000,000	763,865,000,000	1,116,431,000,000
Total, United States	1,407,808,000,000	818,084,000,000	2,225,892,000,000
Percentage 6 public-land States to total United States	25.0	93.3	50.2

[1] Public lands only.

Resources in Tons of Lignite Coal in the Public-Land States

Montana	315,473,043,000
North Dakota	599,945,525,000
South Dakota	1,019,628,000
Washington	500,000

Source: S. Res. 53, 77th Congress, 1st Session, Report No. 838.

Table VIII

War Supply Contracts Compared with the Value of Manufactured Products in 1939

State	War Supply Contracts Through April 1945	Value of Manufactured Products, 1939
Arizona	$ 111,247,000	$ 97,529,481
California	17,595,531,000	2,798,179,523
Colorado	383,854,000	221,642,666
Idaho	17,882,000	90,475,147
Kansas	3,063,994,000	464,353,506
Montana	25,313,000	151,885,026
Nebraska	927,146,000	273,524,581
Nevada	38,090,000	20,581,713
New Mexico	17,578,000	25,123,641
North Dakota	8,187,000	43,767,082
Oregon	1,787,788,000	365,374,436
South Dakota	4,916,000	81,171,887
Utah	107,551,000	167,172,226
Washington	4,555,745,000	636,649,809
Wyoming	65,563,000	45,423,103
Total 15 Western States	28,710,385,000	5,482,853,827
Total U. S.	195,017,437,000	56,843,025,000
Percentage 15 Western States to Total U. S.	15	10

Source: WPB Summary of War Supply and Facility Contracts by State and Industrial Area Cumulative through April 1945, and Statistical Abstract, 1943.

Table IX

Estimated Cost of War Manufacturing Facilities Authorized in the Western States by Important Areas June 1940 Through December 1944

State and Area [1]	Total	Public	Private
Arizona	$ 73,755,000	$ 67,663,000	$ 6,092,000
Phoenix Area	64,025,000	60,917,000	3,108,000
California	1,451,700,000	994,097,000	457,603,000
San Francisco Area	506,561,000	398,796,000	107,765,000
Los Angeles Area	808,145,000	524,546,000	283,599,000
San Diego Area	69,259,000	50,055,000	19,204,000
Colorado	139,464,000	120,671,000	18,793,000
Denver Area	120,507,000	114,108,000	6,399,000
Pueblo Area	13,635,000	5,880,000	7,755,000
Idaho	26,856,000	20,036,000	6,820,000
Pocatello Area	20,548,000	20,036,000	512,000
Kansas	371,676,000	340,402,000	31,274,000
Kansas City Area	192,982,000	179,955,000	13,027,000
Cherokee County	29,477,000	29,357,000	120,000
Douglas County	179,829,000	179,829,000	....
Wichita Area	52,050,000	40,420,000	11,630,000
Montana	6,538,000	77,000	6,461,000
Nebraska	108,038,000	99,691,000	8,347,000
Omaha Area	41,723,000	36,829,000	4,894,000
Grand Island Area	23,461,000	23,416,000	45,000
Saunders County	29,709,000	29,709,000	....
Lincoln Area	7,398,000	5,142,000	2,256,000
Nevada	135,708,000	134,780,000	928,000
Las Vegas Area	135,015,000	134,251,000	764,000
New Mexico	20,812,000	8,543,000	12,269,000
Carlsbad Area	10,269,000	4,059,000	6,210,000
Lea County	5,969,000	2,163,000	3,806,000
North Dakota	2,112,000	120,000	1,992,000
Oregon	124,433,000	93,391,000	31,042,000
Portland Area	100,180,000	83,291,000	16,889,000
Salem Area	9,610,000	5,141,000	4,469,000
South Dakota	1,585,000	150,000	1,435,000
Utah	282,701,000	276,023,000	6,678,000
Provo Area	213,933,000	213,633,000	300,000
Salt Lake City Area	54,522,000	50,526,000	3,996,000
Piute County	5,534,000	5,254,000	280,000
Washington	351,718,000	293,713,000	58,005,000
Seattle Area	146,193,000	128,963,000	17,230,000
Tacoma Area	23,608,000	17,503,000	6,105,000
Spokane Area	101,286,000	100,592,000	694,000
Vancouver Area	51,129,000	31,982,000	19,147,000
Wyoming	31,808,000	23,957,000	7,851,000
Cheyenne Area	12,623,000	12,568,000	55,000
Laramie Area	4,639,000	4,639,000	....
Total 15 Western States	3,128,904,000	2,473,314,000	655,590,000
Total Important Areas	3,033,819,000	2,493,560,000	540,259,000
Total U. S.	21,080,443,000	15,991,993,000	5,088,450,000
Percentage Important Areas to Total U. S.	14.4	15.6	10.6

[1] The value of war manufacturing facilities for the metropolitan areas named are totals of similar figures for the surrounding counties, therefore they do not necessarily check with figures compiled on other bases.

Table X

Important War Plants in Nebraska Financed With Public and Private Funds Through December 31, 1944

Facility Location	Product	Total	Estimated Cost[1] Public	Private
Ammunition	$ 2,837,000	$ 2,837,000	....	Hastings
Meat and meat products	115,000	....	$ 115,000	Cozad
Canned meat products	352,000	....	352,000	Omaha
Dried egg powder	144,000	....	144,000	Omaha
Poultry	419,000	....	419,000	Omaha
Ethyl alcohol, 190 proof	5,751,000	5,751,000	....	Omaha
Dried whole eggs	1,158,000	....	1,158,000	Omaha
Corn Flour Products	524,000	....	524,000	Omaha
Airplanes, B-29 } Airplanes, B-26 }	22,169,000	22,098,000	71,000	Omaha Omaha
Airplane Modification	6,852,000	6,852,000	....	Omaha
Center wing assemblies	517,000	517,000	....	Omaha
Dried eggs	412,000	....	412,000	Omaha
Seaplane derricks } Landing craft, MK 111 }	218,000	144,000	74,000	Omaha
Steel castings	707,000	669,000	38,000	
Whole wheat cereals	193,000	....	193,000	Omaha
Raisin bran	258,000	....	258,000	Omaha
Dry glue, vegetable adhesive liquid	159,000	....	159,000	Omaha
Sausage products, packaged lard	171,000	....	171,000	
Total Omaha	$40,004,000	$36,031,000	$3,973,000	

TABLE X (Continued)

Facility Location	Product	Estimated Cost[1] Total	Public	Private
Ralston	Refinite, zoolite	$ 219,000	....	$ 219,000
Beatrice	Shells	363,000	$ 315,000	48,000
Grand Island	Bomb loading	23,416,000	23,416,000	....
Lincoln	Bomb nose fuses, M 110 motor scooters, gasoline engines, parts	169,000	59,000	110,000
Lincoln	Tank parts	422,000	422,000	....
Lincoln	Self locking elastic stop nuts	4,041,000	2,930,000	1,111,000
Lincoln	Feed mill products	150,000	....	150,000
Lincoln	Self sealing fuel and oil cells, tires, mixed rubber stock	492,000	....	492,000
Lincoln	Inedible fat and tallow	169,000	....	169,000
Lincoln	Milk powder	187,000	94,000	93,000
	Portable telephone and telegraph terminal equipment	1,637,000	1,637,000	....
	Total Lincoln	$ 7,267,000	$ 5,142,000	$2,125,000

Facility Location	Product	Estimated Cost[1] Total	Public	Private
Columbus	Aluminum shapes, tubes, rods and bars and magnesium alloy shapes	1,443,000	1,443,000[2]	....
Crete	Dried eggs and milk, milk processing	126,000	....	126,000
Wahoo	Bomb loading	29,709,000	29,709,000	....
York	Food processing	252,000	....	252,000
	Total Above Cities	$105,751,000	$98,893,000	$6,858,000

[1]Cost of plants over $100,000.
[2]Surplus $1,388,000.

Table XI

IMPORTANT WAR CONTRACTS IN NEBRASKA ACTIVE AS OF JUNE 30, 1945

City	Steel Product	Value of Contract
Ft. Crook	Bomber airplanes, B-29	$270,370,000
Beatrice	Tanks	3,095,000
Beatrice	Munitions	3,159,000
Lincoln	Munitions	4,559,000
Lincoln	Munitions	3,458,000
Lincoln	Telephone and telegraph equipment	9,649,000
Lincoln	Airplane fuel cells	329,000
Wahoo	Bomb loading	26,964,000
Omaha	Steel barges, cart storage cases, ammunition boxes and containers, etc.	5,921,000
Omaha	Munitions	9,518,000
Omaha	Munitions	576,000
Omaha	Soap	482,000
Omaha	Water purifying equipment	733,000
Omaha	Tents	4,742,000
Omaha	Immersion heaters	794,000
	Total above	$344,349,000
	Total Nebraska	$388,949,000

Table XII

Summary of Benefits

	Annual
Irrigation	$ 130,000,000
Power	17,141,000
Flood control	16,500,000
Navigation	4,165,000
Municipal water	500,000
Total	$ 168,306,000
Annual Costs	
Operation, maintenance, repairs, and replacements:	
Irrigation	$ 7,725,000
Power	4,316,000
Flood control and navigation	4,500,000
Amortization of entire cost of project at 3 percent in 50 years	48,872,000
Total annual cost	$ 65,413,000
Ratio of annual costs to annual benefits	1:2.57
Repayments and Returns	
Total estimated cost	$1,257,645,700
Allocation to—	
Flood control	419,300,700
Navigation	97,245,000
Subtotal	516,545,700
Balance repayable	741,100,000
Repayments from—	
Irrigation (40 annual payments)	298,000,000
Power (50 annual payments)[1]	423,100,000
Municipal (40 annual payments)	20,000,000
Total	$ 741,100,000

[1] In addition to the repayments indicated, power revenues will also be sufficient to collect the interest charges on the costs allocated to power.

Source: Bureau of Reclamation Plans for Development of Missouri River Basin, Senate Document No. 191.

TABLE XIII

PROPOSED ELECTRIC POWER PLANTS IN THE MISSOURI RIVER BASIN TO BE OPERATED FOR FIRM POWER

(Jan. 1, 1940 Basis)

	Cost of Construction[1]	Installed Kilowatt Hour	Annual Production, Kilowatt Hour, Firm
Upper Missouri River Basin			
Montana			
Lyon	$ 2,498,000	23,500	121,000,000
Canyon Ferry	11,025,000	35,000	149,800,000
Portage	4,600,000	20,000	146,900,000
Total Area	18,123,000	78,500	417,700,000
Fort Peck to Sioux City Area			
South Dakota			
Oahe	72,800,000	150,000	1,620,600,000 (Oahe, Big Bend, Fort Randall combined)
Big Bend	26,000,000	75,000	
Fort Randall	55,700,000	100,000	
Total South Dakota	154,500,000	325,000	1,620,600,000
Montana			
Fort Peck[2]	10,963,000	35,000	100,700,000
Total Area	165,463,000	360,000	1,721,300,000
Yellowstone Basin			
Montana			
Mission	12,278,000	50,000	263,000,000
Yellowtail	30,289,000	75,000	332,000,000
Total Montana	42,567,000	125,000	595,000,000
Wyoming			
Baysen	8,202,000	10,000	56,900,000
Kane	12,053,000	30,000	139,300,000
Hunter Mountain	8,300,000	12,000	71,000,000
Thief Creek	14,177,000	60,000	350,000,000
Sunlight	3,433,000	20,000	109,500,000
Bald Ridge	7,419,000	30,000	166,500,000
Tongue River[2]	2,375,000	3,000	20,000,000
Total Wyoming	55,959,000	165,000	913,200,000
Total Area	98,526,000	290,000	1,508,200,000
Niobrara, Platte and Kansas River Basin			
Wyoming			
Kortes	5,545,000	30,000	162,000,000
Total Missouri Basin	287,657,000	758,500	3,809,200,000

[1] Dams, reservoirs, and power plants.

[2] Power plant only, does not include reservoir or dam, prorated in proportion to firm or seasonal power.

Source: Bureau of Reclamation Plans for Development of Missouri River Basin, Senate Document No. 191.

Table XIV

Present and Proposed Electric Power Installations in the Missouri Basin

State	Production of Electric Energy in 1941[1] Kilowatt Hours	Proposed Annual Production of Firm Power Kilowatt Hours	Percentage New Power to Present Installations
Montana	2,175,080,000	1,113,400,000	51.2
Wyoming	318,089,000	1,075,200,000	338.0
North Dakota	194,146,000	....	......
South Dakota	182,576,000	1,620,600,000	887.6
Nebraska	918,730,000	....	......
Iowa	216,750,000	....	......
Minnesota	76,200,000	....	......
Total Missouri Basin	4,081,571,000	3,809,200,000	93.3
		Seasonal Power 908,500,000	
Total		4,717,700,000	

[1] Includes publicly and privately owned plants, both hydro and fuel operated.
Source: Bureau of Reclamation Plans for Development of Missouri River Basin. Senate Document No. 191.

SELECTED BIBLIOGRAPHY

GOVERNMENT PUBLICATIONS

THE ALUMINUM INDUSTRY, Report of the Attorney General under Section 205 of the War Mobilization and Reconversion Act of 1944, September, 1945.

MISSOURI RIVER BASIN, Report by the Secretary of the Interior on Bureau of Reclamation's Plan for Basin Development, Senate Document No. 191, 78th Congress, 2nd Session, May, 1944.

MISSOURI RIVER BASIN, Letter from the Secretary of War, transmitting report from the Chief of Engineers, U. S. Army, House Document No. 475, 78th Congress, 2nd Session, March, 1944.

POST-WAR ECONOMIC POLICY AND PLANNING, Report of Senator Jos. C. O'Mahoney to the Special Committee on Post-War Economic Policy and Planning, Senate Document No. 106, 78th Congress, 1st Session, October, 1943.

REPORT OF THE U. S. GREAT PLAINS COMMITTEE, December, 1936.

WESTERN STEEL PLANTS AND THE TIN PLATE INDUSTRY, Report of the Attorney General under Section 205 of the War Mobilization and Reconversion Act of 1944, June, 1945.

INDEX

L

M

N

O

P

R